GOTHIC

In this accessible and lucid introduction Fred Botting traces the sources and developments of a transgressive genre which has thrived for over two centuries. He examines the key texts, origins and writers, as well as their cultural and historical location, their critical reception and their influence.

Gothic focuses on the various styles and forms of the genre and analyses the cultural significance of its prevalent figures: the ghosts, monsters, vampires, doubles and horrors that are its definitive features. Botting traces its history from its origins in the eighteenth century through to modernist and postmodernist representations. He offers a broad overview of the themes, images and effects that not only define the genre but also endure and reappear endlessly in both 'high' and 'popular' literature and culture.

Gothic is an enlightening textbook which students new to the daunting subject of literary theory will find both essential reading and an invaluable foundation for further study.

Fred Botting lectures on Romanticism and literary theory at Lancaster University. He is the author of *Making Monstrous: Frankenstein, Criticism, Theory* and editor of *Frankenstein: A New Casebook*.

THE NEW CRITICAL IDIOM

SERIES EDITOR: JOHN DRAKAKIS, UNIVERSITY OF STIRLING

The New Critical Idiom is an invaluable series of introductory guides to today's critical terminology. Each book:

- provides a handy, explanatory guide to the use (and abuse) of the term

- offers an original and distinctive overview by a leading literary and cultural critic

- relates the term to the larger field of cultural representation.

With a strong emphasis on clarity, lively debate and the widest possible breadth of examples, *The New Critical Idiom* is an indispensable approach to key topics in literary studies.

- See below for new books in this series.

Gothic by Fred Botting
Historicism by Paul Hamilton
Ideology by David Hawkes
Metre, Rhythm and Verse by Philip Hobsbaum
Romanticism by Aidan Day

GOTHIC

Fred Botting

LONDON AND NEW YORK

First published 1996
by Routledge
11 New Fetter Lane, London EC4P 4EE

Simultaneously published in the USA and Canada
by Routledge
29 West 35th Street, New York, NY 10001

Reprinted 1997

Typeset by Keystroke, Jacaranda Lodge, Wolverhampton

Printed and bound in Great Britain by Clays Ltd, St. Ives PLC

British Library Cataloguing in Publication Data
A catalogue record for this book is available from the British Library

Library of Congress Cataloguing in Publication Data
Botting, Fred.
  Gothic / Fred Botting.
    p.   cm. – (The New Critical Idiom)
  Includes bibliographical references.
1. Horror tales. English—History and criticism—Theory, etc.
2. Horror tales, American—History and criticism—Theory, etc.
3. Gothic revival (Literature)—Great Britain.   4. Gothic revival
(Literature)—United States.   5. Literary form.   I. Title.
II. Series.
PR830.T3B68   1996
823'.0872909—dc20   95-7521

ISBN 0–415–13229–0 (hbk)
ISBN 0–415–09219–1 (pbk)

Contents

SERIES EDITOR'S PREFACE

The New Critical Idiom is a series of introductory books which seeks to extend the lexicon of literary terms, in order to address the radical changes which have taken place in the study of literature during the last decades of the twentieth century. The aim is to provide clear, well-illustrated accounts of the full range of terminology currently in use, and to evolve histories of its changing usage.

The current state of the discipline of literary studies is one where there is considerable debate concerning basic questions of terminology. This involves, among other things, the boundaries which distinguish the literary from the non-literary; the position of literature within the larger sphere of culture; the relationship between literatures of different cultures; and questions concerning the relation of literary to other cultural forms within the context of interdisciplinary studies.

It is clear that the field of literary criticism and theory is a dynamic and heterogenous one. The present need is for individual volumes on terms which combine clarity of exposition with an adventurousness of perspective and a breadth of application. Each volume will contain as part of its apparatus some indication of the direction in which the definition of particular terms is likely to move, as well as expanding the disciplinary boundaries within which some of these terms have been traditionally contained. This will involve some re-situation of terms within the larger field of cultural representation, and will introduce examples from the area of film and the modern media in addition to examples from a variety of literary texts.

1

INTRODUCTION
Gothic Excess and Transgression

The language of terror is dedicated to an endless expense, even
though it only seeks to achieve a single effect. It drives itself out of
any possible resting place.
  Sade and the novels of terror introduce an essential imbalance
within works of language: they force them of necessity to be always
excessive and deficient.

(Michel Foucault, 'Language to Infinity', p. 65)

EXCESS

Gothic signifies a writing of excess. It appears in the awful obscurity
that haunted eighteenth-century rationality and morality. It
shadows the despairing ecstasies of Romantic idealism and
individualism and the uncanny dualities of Victorian realism and
decadence. Gothic atmospheres – gloomy and mysterious
– have repeatedly signalled the disturbing return of pasts upon
presents and evoked emotions of terror and laughter. In the
twentieth century, in diverse and ambiguous ways, Gothic figures

have continued to shadow the progress of modernity with counter-narratives displaying the underside of enlightenment and humanist values. Gothic condenses the many perceived threats to these values, threats associated with supernatural and natural forces, imaginative excesses and delusions, religious and human evil, social transgression, mental disintegration and spiritual corruption. If not a purely negative term, Gothic writing remains fascinated by objects and practices that are constructed as negative, irrational, immoral and fantastic. In a world which, since the eighteenth century, has become increasingly secular, the absence of a fixed religious framework as well as changing social and political conditions has meant that Gothic writing, and its reception, has undergone significant transformations. Gothic excesses, none the less, the fascination with transgression and the anxiety over cultural limits and boundaries, continue to produce ambivalent emotions and meanings in their tales of darkness, desire and power.

In Gothic fiction certain stock features provide the principal embodiments and evocations of cultural anxieties. Tortuous, fragmented narratives relating mysterious incidents, horrible images and life-threatening pursuits predominate in the eighteenth century. Spectres, monsters, demons, corpses, skeletons, evil aristocrats, monks and nuns, fainting heroines and bandits populate Gothic landscapes as suggestive figures of imagined and realistic threats. This list grew, in the nineteenth century, with the addition of scientists, fathers, husbands, madmen, criminals and the monstrous double signifying duplicity and evil nature. Gothic landscapes are desolate, alienating and full of menace. In the eighteenth century they were wild and mountainous locations. Later the modern city combined the natural and architectural components of Gothic grandeur and wildness, its dark, labyrinthine streets suggesting the violence and menace of Gothic castle and forest.

The major locus of Gothic plots, the castle, was gloomily predominant in early Gothic fiction. Decaying, bleak and full of hidden passageways, the castle was linked to other medieval edifices – abbeys, churches and graveyards especially – that, in their generally ruinous states, harked back to a feudal past associated with barbarity, superstition and fear. Architecture, particularly medieval in form (although historical accuracy was not a prime concern), signalled the spatial and temporal separation of the past and its values from those of the present. The pleasures of horror and terror came from the reappearance of figures long gone. None the less, Gothic narratives never escaped the concerns of their own times, despite the heavy historical trappings. In later fiction, the castle gradually gave way to the old house: as both building and family line, it became the site where fears and anxieties returned in the present. These anxieties varied according to diverse changes: political revolution, industrialisation, urbanisation, shifts in sexual and domestic organisation, and scientific discovery.

In Gothic productions imagination and emotional effects exceed reason. Passion, excitement and sensation transgress social proprieties and moral laws. Ambivalence and uncertainty obscure single meaning. Drawing on the myths, legends and folklore of medieval romances, Gothic conjured up magical worlds and tales of knights, monsters, ghosts and extravagant adventures and terrors. Associated with wildness, Gothic signified an over-abundance of imaginative frenzy, untamed by reason and unrestrained by conventional eighteenth-century demands for simplicity, realism or probability. The boundlessness as well as the over-ornamentation of Gothic styles were part of a move away from strictly neoclassical aesthetic rules which insisted on clarity and symmetry, on variety encompassed by unity of purpose and design. Gothic signified a trend towards an aesthetics based on feeling and emotion and associated primarily with the sublime.

Throughout the eighteenth century the sublime constituted a major area of debate among writers and theorists of taste. In contrast to beauty, the proportioned contours of which could be taken in by the eye of the beholder, the sublime was associated with grandeur and magnificence. Craggy, mountainous landscapes, the

Alps in particular, stimulated powerful emotions of terror and wonder in the viewer. Their immense scale offered a glimpse of infinity and awful power, intimations of a metaphysical force beyond rational knowledge and human comprehension. In the expansive domain opened up by the sublime all sorts of imaginative objects and fears situated in or beyond nature could proliferate in a marvellous profusion of the supernatural and the ridiculous, the magical and the nightmarish, the fantastic and the absurd.

Linked to poetic and visionary power, the sublime also evoked excessive emotion. Through its presentations of supernatural, sensational and terrifying incidents, imagined or not, Gothic produced emotional effects on its readers rather than developing a rational or properly cultivated response. Exciting rather than informing, it chilled their blood, delighted their superstitious fancies and fed uncultivated appetites for marvellous and strange events, instead of instructing readers with moral lessons that inculcated decent and tasteful attitudes to literature and life. Gothic excesses transgressed the proper limits of aesthetic as well as social order in the overflow of emotions that undermined boundaries of life and fiction, fantasy and reality. Attacked throughout the second half of the eighteenth century for encouraging excessive emotions and invigorating unlicensed passions, Gothic texts were also seen to be subverting the mores and manners on which good social behaviour rested. The feminisation of reading practices and markets, linked to concerns about romances throughout the century, were seen to upset domestic sensibilities as well as sexual propriety. Presenting pasts that the eighteenth century constructed as barbarous or uncivilised, Gothic fictions seemed to promote vice and violence, giving free reign to selfish ambitions and sexual desires beyond the prescriptions of law or familial duty. By nefarious means Gothic villains usurp rightful heirs, rob reputable families of property and reputation while threatening the honour of their wives and orphaned daughters. Illegitimate power and violence is not only put on display but threatens to consume the

world of civilised and domestic values. In the skeletons that leap
from family closets and the erotic and often incestuous tendencies
of Gothic villains there emerges the awful spectre of complete
social disintegration in which virtue cedes to vice, reason to desire,
law to tyranny.

Uncertainties about the nature of power, law, society, family and
sexuality dominate Gothic fiction. They are linked to wider threats
of disintegration manifested most forcefully in political revolution.
The decade of the French Revolution was also the period when
the Gothic novel was at its most popular. Gothic, too, was a
term invoked in many political debates, signifying, for a range
of political positions, revolutionary mobs, enlightened radicals
and irrational adherence to tyrannical and superstitious feudal
values. In a more specific historical sense, Gothic was associated
with the history of the northern, Germanic nations whose fierce
avowal of the values of freedom and democracy was claimed as an
ancient heritage. Opposed to all forms of tyranny and slavery, the
warlike, Gothic tribes of northern Europe were popularly believed
to have brought down the Roman empire. Roman tyranny was
subsequently identified with the Catholic Church, and the production of Gothic novels in northern European Protestant countries
often had an anti-Catholic subtext.

The excesses of political meaning display the ambivalence of
Gothic. In the figures and settings that dominate Gothic narratives
this ambivalence is manifested in terms of the genre's affiliations
with class. Old castles, knights and malevolent aristocrats seem to
fit into an enlightenment pattern identifying all things Gothic
with the tyranny and barbarity of feudal times. Rational distancing
and disavowal of past forms of power, however, is belied by the
continued fascination with the architecture, customs and values of
the Middle Ages: Gothic novels seem to sustain a nostalgic relish
for a lost era of romance and adventure, for a world that, if barbaric, was, from the perspective of the late eighteenth century, also
ordered. In this respect Gothic fiction preserves older traditions

rather than attacking the aristocratic legacy of feudalism. Yet narratives are dominated by values of family, domesticity and virtuous sentimentalism, values more appropriate to the middle-class readership that composed the increasingly large portion of the literary market in the eighteenth century. Aristocratic trappings of chivalry and romance are subsumed by bourgeois values of virtue, merit, propriety and, within reason, individualism. The anxieties about the past and its forms of power are projected on to malevolent and villainous aristocrats in order to consolidate the ascendancy of middle-class values. In nineteenth-century Gothic fiction the trappings of aristocracy, the castles and counts, give way to narratives whose action centres on urban, domestic, commercial and professional figures and locales. Aristocratic excess, though still in evidence, is generally replaced by other forms of threat.

TRANSGRESSION

The excesses and ambivalence associated with Gothic figures were seen as distinct signs of transgression. Aesthetically excessive, Gothic productions were considered unnatural in their under-mining of physical laws with marvellous beings and fantastic events. Transgressing the bounds of reality and possibility, they also challenged reason through their overindulgence in fanciful ideas and imaginative flights. Encouraging superstitious beliefs Gothic narratives subverted rational codes of understanding and, in their presentation of diabolical deeds and supernatural incidents, ventured into the unhallowed ground of necromancy and arcane ritual. The centrality of usurpation, intrigue, betrayal and murder to Gothic plots appeared to celebrate criminal behaviour, violent executions of selfish ambition and voracious passion and licentious enactments of carnal desire. Such terrors, emerging from the gloom of a castle or lurking in the dark features of the villain, were also the source of pleasure, stimulating excitements which blurred definitions of reason and morality and, critics feared, encouraging readers' decline into depravity and corruption. As well as recasting the nature of social and domestic fears, Gothic fictions presented different, more exciting, worlds in which heroines in particular could encounter not only frightening violence but also adventurous freedom. The artificiality of narratives imagined other worlds and also challenged the forms of nature and reality advocated by eighteenth-century social and domestic ideology.

Transgression, like excess, is not simply or lightly undertaken in Gothic fiction, but ambivalent in its aims and effects. Not only a way of producing excessive emotion, a celebration of transgression for its own sake, Gothic terrors activate a sense of the unknown and project an uncontrollable and overwhelming power which threatens not only the loss of sanity, honour, property or social standing but the very order which supports and is regulated by the coherence of those terms. The terrors and horrors of transgression in Gothic writing become a powerful means to reassert the values of society, virtue and propriety: transgression, by crossing the social and aesthetic limits, serves to reinforce or underline their value and necessity, restoring or defining limits. Gothic novels frequently adopt this cautionary strategy, warning of dangers of social and moral transgression by presenting them in their darkest and most threatening form. The tortuous tales of vice, corruption and depravity are sensational examples of what happens when the rules of social behaviour are neglected. Gothic terrors and horrors emanate from readers' identifications with heroes and heroines: after escaping the monsters and penetrating the forest, subterranean or narrative labyrinths of the Gothic nightmare, heroines and readers manage to return with an elevated sense of identity to the solid realities of justice, morality and social order. In political texts of the 1790s like Burke's *Reflections* the construction of revolutionary excesses as a terrifying monster served to define the threat and thus contain and legitimate its exclusion. Terror evoked cathartic emotions and facilitated the expulsion of the object of fear. Transgression, provoking fears of social disintegration, thus enabled the reconstitution of limits and boundaries. Good was affirmed in the contrast with evil; light and reason won out over darkness and superstition. Antitheses, made visible in Gothic transgressions, allowed proper limits and values to be asserted at the closure of narratives in which mysteries were explained or moral resolutions advanced. In an age that developed philosophical, scientific and psychological systems to define and classify the nature of the external world, the parameters of human organisation and their relation to the workings of the mind, transgression is important not only as an interrogation of received rules and values, but in the identification, reconstitution or transformation of limits. In this respect Gothic fiction is less an unrestrained celebration of unsanctioned excesses and more an examination of the limits produced in the eighteenth century to distinguish good from evil, reason from passion, virtue from vice and self from other. Images of light and dark focus, in their duality, the acceptable and unacceptable sides of the limits that regulate social distinctions.

In the demonstrations of the forms and effects of evil by means of terror, the line between transgression and a restitution of acceptable limits remained a difficult one to discern. Some moral endings are little more than perfunctory tokens, thin excuses for salacious excesses, while others sustain a decorous and didactic balance of excitement and instruction. The moral, political and literary ambivalence of Gothic fiction seems to be an effect of the countervailing movements of propriety and imaginative excess in which morality, in its enthusiasm to identify and exclude forms of evil, of culturally threatening elements, becomes entangled in the symbolic and social antagonisms it sets out to distinguish. Defining and affirming one term – reason – by denigrating and excluding the other – passion – moral and literary value admitted both force and emotion as a means of regulating conventional hierarchies. These contradictions undermine the project of attaining and fixing secure boundaries and leave Gothic texts open to a play of ambivalence, a dynamic of limit and transgression that both restores and contests boundaries. This play of terms, of oppositions, indeed, characterises the ambivalence of Gothic fiction: good depends on evil, light on dark, reason on irrationality, in order to define limits. The play means that Gothic is an inscription neither of darkness nor of light, a delineation neither of reason and morality nor of superstition and corruption, neither good nor evil, but both at the same time. Relations between real and fantastic, sacred and profane, supernatural and natural, past and present, civilised and barbaric, rational and fanciful, remain crucial to the Gothic dynamic of limit and transgression.

The play of antitheses produces the ambivalent and excessive effects and reception of Gothic writing. Drawing on various literary forms, Gothic fiction hovers between the categories of novel and romance. Considered as a serious threat to literary and social values, anything Gothic was also discarded as an idle waste of time. Its images of dark power and mystery evoked fear and anxiety, but their absurdity also provoked ridicule and laughter. The emotions most associated with Gothic fiction are similarly ambivalent: objects of terror and horror not only provoke repugnance, disgust and recoil, but also engage readers' interest, fascinating and attracting them. Threats are spiced with thrills, terrors with delights, horrors with pleasures. Terror, in its sublime manifestations, is associated with subjective elevation, with the pleasures of imaginatively transcending or overcoming fear and thereby renewing and heightening a sense of self and social value: threatened with dissolution, the self, like the social limits which define it, reconstitutes its identity against the otherness and loss presented in the moment of terror. The subjective elevation in moments of terror is thus exciting and pleasurable, uplifting the self by means of emotional expenditure that simultaneously excludes the object of fear. In the process, fear and its darkly obscure object is externalised and limits are reconstituted between inside and outside. While terror and horror are often used synonymously, distinctions can be made between them as countervailing aspects of Gothic's emotional ambivalence. If terror leads to an imaginative expansion of one's sense of self, horror describes the movement of contraction and recoil. Like the dilation of the pupil in moments of excitement and fear, terror marks the uplifting thrill where horror distinguishes a contraction at the imminence and unavoidability of the threat. Terror expels after horror glimpses invasion, reconstituting the boundaries that horror has seen dissolve.

The movement between terror and horror is part of a dynamic whose poles chart the extent and different directions of Gothic projects. These poles, always inextricably linked, involve the externalisation or internalisation of objects of fear and anxiety. The different movements implied by terror and horror characterise the most important shift in the genre. In the eighteenth century the emphasis was placed on expelling and objectifying threatening figures of darkness and evil, casting them out and restoring proper limits: villains are punished; heroines well married. In the nineteenth century, the security and stability of social, political and aesthetic formations are much more uncertain. In the changing political and philosophical conditions attendant on the French Revolution all hierarchies and distinctions governing social and economic formations were in question. Gothic castles, villains and ghosts, already made clichéd and formulaic by popular imitation, ceased to evoke terror or horror. Their capacity to embody and externalise fears and anxieties was in decline. If they remained, they continued more as signs of internal states and conflicts than of external threats. The new concern inflected in Gothic forms emerged as the darker side to Romantic ideals of individuality, imaginative consciousness and creation. Gothic became part of an internalised world of guilt, anxiety, despair, a world of individual transgression interrogating the uncertain bounds of imaginative freedom and human knowledge. Romantic ideals were shadowed by Gothic passions and extravagance. External forms were signs of psychological disturbance, of increasingly uncertain subjective states dominated by fantasy, hallucination and madness. The internalisation of Gothic forms reflected wider anxieties which, centring on the individual, concerned the nature of reality and society and its relation to individual freedom and imagination. Terror became secondary to horror, the sublime ceded to the uncanny, the latter an effect of uncertainty, of the irruption of fantasies, suppressed wishes and emotional and sexual conflicts. A disruptive return of archaic desires and fears, the uncanny disturbs the familiar, homely and secure sense of reality and normality. The disturbance of psychic states, however, does not signal a purely subjective disintegration: the uncanny renders all boundaries uncertain and, in nineteenth-century Gothic writing, often leaves readers unsure whether narratives describe psychological disturbance or wider upheavals within formations of reality and normality.

Less identifiable as a separate genre in the nineteenth century, Gothic fiction seemed to go underground: its depths were less romantic chasms or labyrinthine dungeons, than the murky recesses of human subjectivity. The city, a gloomy forest or dark labyrinth itself, became a site of nocturnal corruption and violence, a locus of real horror; the family became a place rendered threatening and uncanny by the haunting return of past transgressions and attendant guilt on an everyday world shrouded in strangeness. The attempt to distinguish the apparent from the real, the good from the bad, evident in the standard Gothic device of portraits assuming life, was internalised rather than explained as a supernatural occurrence, a trick of the light or of the imagination. Uncanny effects rather than sublime terrors predominated. Doubles, *alter egos*, mirrors and animated representations of the disturbing parts of human identity became the stock devices. Signifying the alienation of the human subject from the culture and language in which s/he was located, these devices increasingly destabilised the boundaries between psyche and reality, opening up an indeterminate zone in which the differences between fantasy and actuality were no longer secure.

The Gothic strain existed in excess of, and often within, realist forms, both inhabiting and excluded from its homogenising representations of the world. Psychological rather than supernatural forces became the prime movers in worlds where individuals could be sure neither of others nor of themselves. As bourgeois modes of social organisation and economic and aesthetic production demanded increasing realism, self-discipline and regulation of its individuals, with techniques being developed by social and scientific practices, those persons that deviated from its norms became fascinating objects of scrutiny. Gothic subjects were alienated, divided from themselves, no longer in control of those passions, desires, and fantasies, that had been policed and partially expunged in the eighteenth century. Individuals were divided products of both reason and desire, subjects of obsession, narcissism and self-gratification as much as reasonable, responsible codes of behaviour. Nature, wild and untameable, was as much within as without. Excess emanated from within, from hidden, pathological motivations that rationality was powerless to control. Scientific theory and technological innovation, often used as figures of human alienation and Gothic excess themselves, provided a vocabulary and objects of fear and anxiety for nineteenth-century Gothic writing. Darwinian models of evolution, researches in criminology, anatomical and physiological science identified the bestial within the human. Categorised forms of deviance and abnormality explained criminal behaviour as a pathological return of animalistic, instinctual habits. The forms of history deployed, appearing like ghosts in the present, were less feudal and romantic and more an effect of scientific discourse: guilts and fears haunted individuals and families, while primal patterns of instinct and motivation threatened the humanity of the human species. Science, with its chemical concoctions, mechanical laboratories and electrical instruments became a new domain for the encounter with dark powers, now secular, mental and animal rather than supernatural. Crime similarly presented a challenge to rationality in a degenerate world of mysterious but distinctly human and corrupt motivations. In defining a divided world of divided beings, science also disclosed a sense of loss, of the decline of human society and its values of individual strength and health. Faced with this loss, presented as social degeneration, criminal and sexual degradation, science gave way to a new spirituality which tried to recover a sense of cultural value and unity by inflecting science with sacred, religious powers, powers that invoked conventional Gothic figures and strategies.

DIFFUSION

Many of the anxieties articulated in Gothic terms in the nineteenth century reappear in the twentieth century. Their appearance, however, is more diverse, a diffusion of Gothic traces among a multiplicity of different genres and media. Science fiction, the adventure novel, modernist literature, romantic fiction and popular horror writing often resonate with Gothic motifs that have been transformed and displaced by different cultural anxieties. Terror and horror are diversely located in alienating bureaucratic and technological reality, in psychiatric hospitals and criminal subcultures, in scientific, future and intergalactic worlds, in fantasy and the occult. Threatening figures of menace, destruction and violence emerge in the form of mad scientists, psychopaths, extraterrestrials and a host of strange supernatural or naturally monstrous mutations.

One place, however, has perpetuated distinctly Gothic figures: the cinema. From the 1930s vampires, Jekylls and Hydes, Frankensteins and monsters have populated cinema and television screens in a variety of guises ranging from the seriously sinister to the comic and ridiculous. Their popularity, as well as the way they ambivalently reflect cultural anxieties, locates them firmly in the non-literary, cultural, tradition that conventionally remains the true locus of Gothic.

On the screen as well as in certain novels, Gothic narratives display a more serious 'literary' or self-conscious aspect. In this respect they echo the concerns about narrative that are embedded in Gothic writing from its beginnings, concerns about the limits, effects and power of representation in the formation of identities, realities and institutions. Gothic devices are all signs of the superficiality, deception and duplicity of narratives and verbal or visual images. In a century that has become increasingly sceptical about the values and practices associated with modernity and perceives these values as powerful fictions or grand narratives, new and yet familiar terrors and horrors emerge to present the dissolution of all order, meaning and identity in a play of signs, images and texts. One of the principal horrors lurking throughout Gothic fiction is the sense that there is no exit from the darkly illuminating labyrinth of language.

The diffusion of Gothic forms and figures over more than two centuries makes the definition of a homogeneous generic category exceptionally difficult. Changing features, emphases and meanings disclose Gothic writing as a mode that exceeds genre and categories, restricted neither to a literary school nor to a historical period. The diffusion of Gothic features across texts and historical periods distinguishes the Gothic as a hybrid form, incorporating and transforming other literary forms as well as developing and changing its own conventions in relation to newer modes of writing. In many ways the multiple origins of Gothic writing highlight its diverse composition. While certain devices and plots, what might be called the staples of the Gothic, are clearly identifiable in early Gothic texts, the tradition draws on medieval romances, supernatural, Faustian and fairy tales, Renaissance drama, sentimental, picaresque and confessional narratives as well as the ruins, tombs and nocturnal speculations that fascinated Graveyard poets.

Apart from the period in which the key Gothic texts were produced, a period extending from Horace Walpole's *The Castle of Otranto* (1764) to Charles Maturin's *Melmoth the Wanderer* (1820), it is impossible to define a fixed set of conventions. Even these dates seem arbitrary, straddling as they do the eras dominated by neoclassical and Romantic writing. Gothic forms, moreover, are not only shaped by literatures of the past: the styles prevailing in the respective presents in which they were produced also provide their specific shape. Nowhere is this more evident than in the shifts that occurred within Gothic writing in the move from a neoclassical to a Romantic context, and in the various, and differently marked, descriptions of texts as novels, romances or tales. Gothic writing emerges and takes shape in relation to dominant literary practices, a relationship that is as much antithetical as imitative. In the changes of Gothic sites of terror and horror in the nineteenth century, uncanny shadows were cast on the privileged loci of realism.

Existing in relation to other forms of writing, Gothic texts have generally been marginalised, excluded from the sphere of acceptable literature. Their popularity within an expanding readership in the eighteenth and nineteenth centuries, as novels borrowed a volume at a time from circulating libraries or in the form of stories in the periodical magazines that indulged the appetite for tales of terror or as burlesques and melodramas produced for the stage, was a clear sign of their tastelessness and vulgarity. In the realm of popular culture, however, Gothic writing thrived and exerted an influence on more properly literary forms. From the high cultural position associated with Literature, Gothic not only signified popular fiction but remained a darker undercurrent to the literary tradition itself. That tradition, however, distinguishing itself and its canon of great works according to different codes and values in specific periods, remains discontinuous and partial. What might, loosely, be called the Gothic tradition, is no less partial and fragmented. It possesses, however, a broad, if strange, continuity in the way it draws inspiration, plots and techniques from medieval romances and poetry, from ballads and folklore, from Renaissance writing, especially Shakespearean drama and Spenserian poetry, as well as from various seventeenth- and eighteenth-century prose forms. Articulating different, popular and often marginalised forms of writing in periods and genres privileged as Romanticism, Realism and Modernism, Gothic writing emerges as the thread that defines British literature. In the United States, where the literary canon is composed of works in which the influence of romances and Gothic novels is far more overt, literature again seems virtually an effect of a Gothic tradition. Gothic can perhaps be called the only true literary tradition. Or its stain.

This introductory volume examines the distinctive features, particular types and significant transformations of the genre. It looks at Gothic's relation to other genres by selecting key texts from the diverse range of material from the eighteenth century to the present. The amount of material, given not only the number and variety of texts but their different textual and cultural conditions of production, has necessitated certain omissions in order that particular examples of Gothic writing can be located and analysed in specific contexts. The focus is primarily on Gothic writing in English: there are no discussions of Russian texts, nor of French productions, despite the Gothic elements that appear in some symbolist and surrealist work. In part this is because lines of connection are difficult to trace: the surrealist interest in Gothic texts is indirect, appearing to stem from a deeper fascination with the work of the Marquis de Sade who, in his 'Reflections on the Novel', praised Mrs Radcliffe's and M. G. Lewis's narratives. German tales, given the widespread popular association of Gothic with all things gloomy and Germanic, receive only brief attention in references to the influence of German Romanticism, particularly of E. T. A. Hoffman and Ludwig Tieck, on British and American writing. Focusing on particular texts as representative of Gothic developments in the eighteenth, nineteenth and twentieth centuries, the discussions of Gothic texts analyse the generic diffusion of Gothic forms, especially in the twentieth century. Moreover, addressing recent or postmodern texts in the light of Gothic features presents uncanny parallels between the 1790s, 1890s and 1990s and facilitates a rereading of the narratives of modernity.

CRITICISM

The approach of this book has been made possible by recent developments and re-examinations in literary, critical and cultural theory. This is not to say, however, that earlier scholarship and critical enthusiasm for Gothic writing has been neglected, far from it. While work of this kind sustained serious interest in forms marginalised, if not forgotten, by canons as curiosities in the history of literary production and consumption, the shift in values and perspectives provided by recent theories has significantly altered attitudes to Gothic texts. By challenging the hierarchies of literary value and widening the horizons of critical study to include other forms of writing and address different cultural and historical issues, recent critical practices have moved Gothic texts from previously marginalised sites designated as popular fiction or literary eccentricity. The questioning of boundaries in recent criticism is highly appropriate to studies of Gothic texts.

This introductory volume draws on the different issues and perspectives informing and structuring critical interpretations and reinterpretations: it is an effect of previous writing, a selective composite of various critical readings which, while referring to no specific critical statement other than those by contemporary reviewers, remains indebted to the history of Gothic criticism. The most informative work on different aspects of Gothic writing and using different approaches is cited in the bibliography.

The following overview will indicate the variety of ways criticism has engaged with Gothic writing, engagements that are clearly affected by changing critical positions. In the early part of the twentieth century, from the 1920s, Gothic writing was discussed as a subgenre, of peripheral interest as part of general literary historical surveys discussing the development of the novel. Michael Sadleir's interest was a result of the list of 'horrid' novels cited in Jane Austen's *Northanger Abbey* (1818). In J. M. S. Tompkins's study of the popular novel various themes and characteristics of Gothic were situated within a general literary historical context, while Edith Birkhead examined particular tales more closely in terms of their literary merit. More favourable accounts of Gothic novels were offered in Montague Summers's, and subsequently Devendra Varma's, critical histories. The appeal, for them, of Gothic writing lay in its opposition to realism and rationalism, in its quest for a realm beyond the empirical and material world, for a realm of the mysterious, mystical and holy. For them, terror and horror are linked to awe and dread as ways of representing a human quest for metaphysical, religious experience in a secular age. While, in *The Gothic Quest* (1938), Summers traced Gothic influences into the twentieth century, it is in examining the classical Gothic texts and in Romanticism that his work holds most interest. He initiated attempts at classifying different Gothic texts. Categories of 'supernatural-', 'historical-', 'rational-' and 'terror-Gothic' have, since Summers, been amended in Varma's work, in G. R. Thompson's collections, and in Robert Hume's and Robert Platzner's debate, in order to account for different Gothic features and effects, especially that of horror.

Much of this critical work focuses on the relation between Gothic and Romantic writing. Broader definitions of Romanticism, like those by Eino Railo and Mario Praz, include Gothic writings, but as examples of less ideal themes of violence, incest, passion and agony: Gothic becomes the dark or negative side to Romanticism. In the contrasts displayed in Gothic presentations of darker themes, criticism finds an explicit invitation to indulge in traditional psychoanalysis: Gothic becomes a fiction of unconscious desire, a release of repressed energies and antisocial fantasies. Themes of the divided nature of the human constitution have become established ways of discussing Gothic texts: dualities of mind and body, reason and desire, are repeatedly invoked. Popular Freudianism, assimilated by nineteenth-century notions of human duality, is ubiquitous, informing texts like Robert Kiely's and Masao Miyoshi's on the romantic novel and the divided self.

David Punter's exhaustive survey of Gothic literature is similarly Freudian, though heavily tempered by Marxist criticism. Punter's analysis, like Franco Moretti's accounts of *Frankenstein* and *Dracula*, focuses on issues of class by relating Gothic texts to anxieties about aristocratic and bourgeois power, as well as the fears about the monstrous proletariat and forms of alienation. Since de Sade's 'Reflections on the Novel', Gothic has been linked to revolutionary energies, a connection recently examined by Ronald Paulson. With Ellen Moers's notion of 'female Gothic' as a mode of addressing fears about sexuality and childbirth, one of the most significant directions in recent Gothic criticism was laid out. A challenge to, or interrogation of, forms of fiction dominated by patriarchal assumptions, Gothic novels have been reassessed as part of a wider feminist critical movement that recovers suppressed or marginalised writing by women and addresses issues of female experience, sexual oppression and difference.

Extensive interrogations of traditional literary and cultural institutions, related to those enunciated in Marxist and feminist criticism, have emerged in the wake of structuralist theory. Stressing the role of linguistic structures and differences in the formation of cultural meanings, post-structuralist criticisms have attended to relations of textual, sexual and historical production and reproduction. Eve Kosofsky Sedgwick's book on Gothic conventions disclosed the textuality of the genre, the play of narrative surfaces and metaphors that undermine assumptions of depth and hidden meaning. The link between textuality, power and desire in Gothic fiction has been theorised by Jerrold Hogle, and a recent book,

Gothic Writing (1993), by Robert Miles has examined the discursive frameworks enabling the production of earlier Gothic writing. Several critical essays on specific Gothic texts have begun to interpret the genre's relation to notions of identity, sexuality, power and imperialism. Indeed, from the eighteenth century onwards, Gothic texts have been involved in constructing and contesting distinctions between civilisation and barbarism, reason and desire, self and other.

Gothic excesses and transgressions repeatedly return to particular images and particular loci. Familial and sexual relations, power and suppression, turn on the roles and figures of father and daughter. In villains, masculine sovereignty is staged and scrutinised. Old castles, houses and ruins, as in wild landscapes and labyrinthine cities, situate heroines and readers at the limits of normal worlds and mores. Historical events or imagined pasts, also, delineate the boundaries of the normalised present in a movement, an interplay, that leaves neither where they were. In its crossing of boundaries, however, Gothic is a mobile and specific form. For the images and figures that are reiterated constitute a place where cultural fears and fantasies are projected. Thus similar figures have different significances, depending on the culture that uses them. Indeed, this is the pattern of Gothic as a genre that, in generating and refracting diverse objects of fear and anxiety, transforms its own shape and focus. In structuring this book along conventional chronological lines, cultural and historical discontinuities as well as continuities can be plotted, demonstrating the major shifts in Gothic production as well as the persistence of certain patterns. Drawing on newer critical work as well as earlier studies, this introduction anticipates future examinations of the ways Gothic texts produce, reinforce and undermine received ideas about literature, nation, gender and culture.

2

GOTHIC ORIGINS

Lust, murder, incest, and every atrocity that can disgrace human nature, brought together, without the apology of probability, or even possibility for their introduction. To make amends, the moral is general and *very practical*; it is, 'not to deal in witchcraft and magic because the devil will have you at last!!' We are sorry to observe that good talents have been misapplied in the production of this monster.

(The British Critic 7, June 1796, p. 677)

Morality and monstrosity were two of the hallmarks of eighteenth-century aesthetic judgement. The lack of the former and abundance of the latter, in the eyes of the reviewer for the *British Critic* (1796), distinguished M. G. Lewis's *The Monk* as a particularly deserving object of critical vitriol. The review is not extraordinary either in the tone it adopts or in the terms it employs, though *The Monk* achieved special notoriety. While a few writers, now established as founders of the Gothic tradition – Horace Walpole and Ann Radcliffe particularly – received both critical and popular approbation, they were in the minority. Between 1790 and 1810 critics were almost univocal in their condemnation of what was seen as an unending torrent of popular trashy novels. Intensified by fears of radicalism and revolution, the challenge to aesthetic values was framed in terms of social transgression: virtue, propriety and domestic order were considered to be under threat.

However, the basis for rejections of Gothic novels had been laid much earlier in the century. The values that gave shape and direction to the Enlightenment, dominated as it was by writings from Greek and Roman culture, privileged forms of cultural or artistic production that attended to the classical rules. Buildings, works of art, gardens, landscapes and written texts had to conform to precepts of uniformity, proportion and order. Aesthetic objects were praised for their harmony and texts were designed to foster appreciation on these terms, to instruct rather than entertain, to inculcate a sense of morality and rational understanding and thus educate readers in the discrimination of virtue and vice. Taste, judgement and value were predicated on ideas of cultivation and civilised behaviour that were entwined with social mores of public and domestic duty, harmony and propriety. The dominance of classical values produced a national past that was distinct from the cultivation, rationality and maturity of an enlightened age. This past was called 'Gothic', a general and derogatory term for the Middle Ages which conjured up ideas of barbarous customs and practices, of superstition, ignorance, extravagant fancies and natural wildness. Manifestations of the Gothic past – buildings, ruins, songs and romances – were treated as products of unculti-vated if not childish minds. But characteristics like extravagance, superstition, fancy and wildness which were initially considered in negative terms became associated, in the course of the eighteenth century, with a more expansive and imaginative potential for aesthetic production.

Gothic productions never completely lost their earlier, negative connotations to become fully assimilated within the bounds of proper literature. Implicated in a major shift in cultural attitudes,

Gothic works came to harbour a disturbing ambivalence which disclosed the instability not only of modes of representation but also of the structures that held those representations in place. Throughout the century important social, economic and political as well as cultural changes began to prise apart the bonds linking individuals to an ordered social world. Urbanisation, industrialisation, revolution were the principal signs of change. Enlightenment rationalism displaced religion as the authoritative mode of explaining the universe and altered conceptions of the relations between individuals and natural, supernatural and social worlds. Gothic works and their disturbing ambivalence can thus be seen as effects of fear and anxiety, as attempts to account for or deal with the uncertainty of these shifts. They are also attempts to explain what the Enlightenment left unexplained, efforts to reconstruct the divine mysteries that reason had begun to dismantle, to recuperate pasts and histories that offered a permanence and unity in excess of the limits of rational and moral order. In this respect the past that was labelled Gothic was a site of struggle between enlightened forces of progress and more conservative impulses to retain continuity. The contest for a coherent and stable account of the past, however, produced an ambivalence that was not resolved. The complex and often contradictory attempts either to make the past barbaric in contrast to an enlightened present or to find in it a continuity that gave English culture a stable history had the effect of bringing to the fore and transforming the way in which both past and present depended on modes of representation.

The various developments in aesthetic practice that paved the way for Gothic fiction are themselves accompanied by similar concerns about the nature and effects of representation. Romances, the tales of magical occurrences and exotic adventures that drew on the customs and superstitions of the Middle Ages, met, from the late seventeeth century on, with general disapproval. Graveyard poetry, rejecting human vices and vanities through an insistence on mortality, encouraged an interest in ruins, tombs and nocturnal gloom as the frontiers that opened on to an afterlife of infinite bliss. The taste for the sublime that dominated eighteenth-century aesthetic enquiries also offered intimations of an infinity beyond the limits of any rational framework. Natural and artistic objects were seen to evoke emotional effects like terror and wonder which marked an indistinct sense of an immensity that exceeded human comprehension and elevated human sensibility. The effusive and imaginative descriptions of objects both natural and supernatural that were recovered by scholars collecting the songs and ballads of medieval culture provided the examples of a romantic and sublime way of writing. Similarly, medieval architecture, with its cathedrals, castles and ruins, became a worthy model for evocations of sublimity.

The Gothic novel owes much to these developments. The marvellous incidents and chivalric customs of romances, the descriptions of wild and elemental natural settings, the gloom of the graveyard and ruin, the scale and permanence of the architecture, the terror and wonder of the sublime, all become important features of the eighteenth-century Gothic novel. Similarly, the emphasis on the limits of the neoclassical aesthetic project that occurs in reappraisals of romances, ruins and sublimity provides an important stimulus to the imaginative aspirations of Gothic fiction.

ROMANCE AND NOVEL

In discussions of eighteenth-century fiction, the term 'Gothic romance' is more applicable than 'Gothic novel' as it highlights the link between medieval romances, the romantic narratives of love, chivalry and adventure, that were imported from France from the late seventeenth century onwards, and the tales that in the later eighteenth century were classified as 'Gothic'. Neoclassical criticism throughout the eighteenth century found much to disapprove of, often without any attempt at discrimination, in novels and romances. Works of fiction were subjected to general condemnation as wildly fanciful pieces of folly that served no useful or moral purpose.

In a review of Smollett's *Peregrine Pickle* (1751), one critic, John Cleland, complained:

> Serious and useful works are scarce read, and hardly any thing of morality goes down, unless ticketed with the label of amusement. Hence that flood of novels, tales, romances, and other monsters of the imagination, which have been either wretchedly translated, or even more unhappily imitated, from the *French*, whose literary levity we have not been ashamed to adopt, and to encourage the propagation of so depraved a taste.

Instead, the precepts of classical writers like Horace and Plutarch are recommended. Writing from life is considered the morally instructive way to ward off 'monsters of the imagination', providing guidance in the ways of the world rather than extravagant excursions of the imagination:

> For as the matter of them is taken chiefly from nature, from adventures, real or imaginary, but familiar, practical and probable to be met with in the course of common life, they may serve as pilot's charts, or maps of those parts of the world, which every one may chance to travel through; and in this light they are public benefits. Whereas romances and novels which turn upon characters out of nature, monsters of perfection, feats of chivalry, fairy-enchantments, and the whole train of the marvellously absurd, transport the reader unprofitably into the clouds, where he is sure to find no solid footing, or into those wilds of fancy, which go for ever out of the way of all human paths.

It was not only the failure to attend to rules of imitation that proved to be an object of critical concern. The straying of fancy from the paths of nature demonstrated more than a depraved taste:

it was also believed to exert a corrupting influence on the morals of readers. Complaining at the 'deluge of familiar romances', T. Row observed in the *Gentleman's Magazine* (1767): ''Tis not only a most unprofitable way of spending time, but extremely predjudicial to their morals, many a young person being entirely corrupted by the giddy and fantastical notions of love and gallantry, imbibed from thence'. Indeed, the danger of moral degeneration became the principal reason for the general condemnation of romances, tales and novels.

Despite the prevailing indiscriminate dismissal of romances and novels, attempts were made to distinguish between modes of fictional writing and to admit a few examples of the latter within the parameters of acceptability. James Beattie's 'On Fable and Romance' (1783) draws clear distinctions between medieval romances and novels. The essay argues that Cervantes' *Don Quixote* signals the end of the old or medieval romance and the emergence of the modern romance or novel: 'Fiction henceforth divested herself of her gigantick size, tremendous aspect, and frantick demeanour; and, descending to the level of common life, conversed with man as his equal, and as a polite and cheerful companion.' From Cervantes, writers learnt 'to avoid extravagance, and imitate nature' by adhering to rules of probability (Williams, p. 320). Novels are divided into serious and comic forms. Included, with some approval, in these categories are works by writers who are now regarded as the core of the eighteenth-century novel tradition: Defoe, Richardson, Fielding and Smollett. However, Beattie's essay concludes on a cautionary and, by 1783, a conventional note, describing romances as 'a dangerous recreation' of which a few 'may be friendly to good taste and good morals' while the majority 'tend to corrupt the heart, and stimulate the passions'. 'A habit of reading them', Beattie goes on, 'breeds a dislike to history, and all the substantial parts of knowledge; withdraws the attention from nature, and truth; and fills the mind with extravagant thoughts, and too often with criminal propensities'

(Williams, p. 327). Beattie's warning about romances echoes the distinctions that grounded eighteenth-century criticism: in the maintenance of morality, propriety and virtue, truth, reason, knowledge and taste should always be elevated above fiction, passion, ignorance and depravity.

In *The Rambler* (1750), Samuel Johnson differentiated between romances and novels in similar terms. But he was also keen to stress the moral usefulness of the latter. Romances were described as wildly extravagant and fanciful tales of knights, giants, fabulous entities and marvellous incidents. Novels were privileged as instructive observations on the living world. It was, however, more than accurate imitation of nature or polite society that separated good writing from bad. For Johnson, the 'familiar histories' offered by novels possessed the capacity to educate readers, to convey with greater efficiency a knowledge of virtue and vice. The realism of novels, moreover, was required to be selective: imitations of nature and life were to be chosen on the basis of their propriety and not be coloured by passion or wickedness. Novels ought to highlight virtue and elicit a reader's abhorrence at depictions of vice. The reason for the representation of vice is made clear in lines from Pope's *Essay on Man*: 'Vice is a monster of so frightful mien/As, to be hated, needs but to be seen' (II, 217–18).

Representations of vice as a monster conformed to an important strategy in that it defined the limits of propriety. The term monster also applied in aesthetic judgements to works that were unnatural and deformed, that deviated either from the regularity attributed to life and nature or from the symmetry and proportion valued in any form of representation. Thus it was less a matter of concern that monsters were represented and more a question of the manner in which they were represented and of the effects of those representations. Romances were easily categorised as examples of childish fancy, trivial and incredible tales of ignorance and superstition. Their effects on readers, however, were of major concern. In encouraging readers' credulity and imagination, and in blurring the boundaries between supernatural and illusory dimensions and natural and real worlds, romances loosened the moral and rational structures that ordered everyday life. By displaying monsters in too attractive a light, vice rather than virtue might be promoted. For, if fiction, as Johnson maintained, should establish and reproduce moral and proper ideas of conduct, it could also become a manual of misconduct.

Fiction was thus recognised as a powerful but ambivalent form of social education. The insistence on distinctions between romances and novels forms part of a wider process of teaching readers proper moral and rational understanding. Distinguishing between good and bad modes of writing was more than a merely aesthetic enterprise: it marked an attempt to supplement an assumed inability on the part of romances and their growing readership to discriminate between virtue and vice, and thus to forestall their seduction along fictional paths that stimulated antisocial passions and corrupt behaviour. That these boundaries were difficult to police accounts for the repeated critical effort to maintain them. Even the clear classifications proposed by Beattie and Johnson fell foul of the way in which their terms were framed. Beattie's essay on medieval romances and the novel form describes another type as a 'strange mixture' of the two. As examples, Beattie cites texts by the late seventeenth-century French writer Madeleine de Scudery which he goes on to describe:

> In them, all facts and characters, real and fabulous; and systems of policy and manners, the Greek, the Roman, the Feudal, and the modern, are jumbled together and confounded: as if a painter should represent Julius Cesar drinking tea with Queen Elizabeth, Jupiter, and Dulcinea del Toboso, and having on his head the laurel wreathe of antient Rome, a suit of Gothick armour on his shoulders, laced ruffles at his wrist, a pipe of tobacco in his mouth, and a pistol and tomahawk stuck in his belt.
>
> (Williams, p. 320)

The diversity of events, styles, settings and characters composing this strange assemblage engages in an extravagant refusal to respect boundaries of fact and fiction and reproduce imitations of nature and life. As a result they are rejected as 'intolerably tedious' and 'unspeakably absurd'. These romances, however, are the fore-runners of the strange mixture of forms that appeared as Gothic tales later in the century. Indeed, while at Eton, Horace Walpole described the effects of his predilection for romances in a letter to George Montagu (6 May 1736): 'As I got farther into Virgil and *Clelia*, I found myself transported from Arcadia, to the garden of Italy, and saw Windsor Castle in no other view than the *capitoli immobile saxum.*'

The word 'romance' had come to signify more recent produc-tions as well as medieval narratives. Charlotte Lennox's novel *The Female Quixote* (1752) satirises romance reading by presenting a heroine who interprets every event as though it were part of some great romantic adventure. Despite critical and novelistic attempts to sustain distinctions, fiction continued to upset conventions of reading and codes of behaviour. Even forceful attempts, like Johnson's, to mark out the useful and moral from the wasteful and corrupting potential of fiction encountered the destabilising pleasures of writing. In her *The Progress of Romance* (1785), Clara Reeve, herself a writer of Gothic and historical romances, outlined in very Johnsonian terms a definition of romance and novel while acknowledging the seductive power of fiction:

> The Romance is an heroic fable, which treats of fabulous persons and things. – The Novel is a picture of real life and manners, and of the times in which it is written. The Romance in lofty and elevated language, describes what never happened or is likely to happen. – The Novel gives a familiar relation of such things, as pass every day before our eyes, such as may happen to our friend, or to ourselves; and the perfection of it, is to represent every scene, in so easy and natural a manner,

> and to make them appear so probable, as to deceive us into a
> persuasion (at least while we are reading) that all is real, until
> we are affected by the joys or distresses, of the persons in the
> story, as if they were our own.
>
> (I, p. 111)

In deceiving readers with persuasively real representations of events
and characters, novels work in an opposite manner to romances.
The concern about the effects of fiction becomes paramount in
eighteenth-century criticism. That these are representations is not
at issue. What is more important are the values that are reproduced
as natural or real rather than the actual form of nature or everyday
life. Fiction becomes distinctly, though ambivalently, ideological.
Able to reproduce a set of dominant ideas about the relationship of
individuals to their social and natural world, all narratives were
acknowledged, if only at times tacitly, to possess the capacity to
order or subvert manners, morals and perceptions.

   In the response to Gothic architecture, too, the operations
of enlightenment ideology are apparent. Privileging uniformity
and proportion over scale and extravagance, eighteenth-century
critics classified any deviations from symmetrical structure as the
deformities exhibited by the absence of taste of a barbaric age.
Neve's *Complete Builder's Guide* (1703) dismisses medieval edifices
as 'massive, cumbersome and unwieldy'. In contrast Elizabethan
imitations of Gothic structure were characterised by their 'affected
lightness, Delicacy, and over-rich, even whimsical Decorations'
(Clark, pp. 50–1). As in criticism of romances, chronological
differences tended to be elided so any constructions that were
wastefully over-ornamented or unwielding and cumbersome were
described as Gothic. Comparisons between Gothic and classical
architecture served only to display the superiority of the latter.
Joseph Addison, for example, praised the great and amazing form
of the Pantheon in Rome and contrasted it with the meanness he
found in Gothic cathedrals. Alexander Gerard, in his *Essay on Taste*
(1764), denied Gothic structures any claim to beauty because they

lacked proportion and simplicity (Monk, pp. 34–5). Lord Kames, in his *Elements of Criticism* (1762), clearly states prevailing attitudes towards beautiful form: 'viewing any body as a whole, the beauty of its figure arises from regularity and simplicity; viewing the parts in relation to each other, uniformity, proportion and order, contribute to its beauty' (p. 85).

The insistence on neoclassical rules of composition manifests the importance attached to the manner in which eighteenth-century culture constructed and reproduced its own idea of itself. Architecture told the story of its development and represented its values; it was interpreted accordingly. Some of Kames's apparently inconsequential speculations on the appropriate architectural style of ruins indicate a certain investment in distancing the enlightened present from a Gothic past: 'Whether should a ruin be in the Gothic or Grecian form? In the former, I think; because it exhibits the triumph of time over strength; a melancholy but not un-pleasant thought: a Grecian ruin suggests rather the triumph of barbarity over taste; a gloomy and discouraging thought' (p. 430). This somewhat fastidious way of accounting for the appropriate taste displays a serious effort to privilege classical cultivation over the barbarity of the past. Any deviation from the standards of the present, any sign of imperfection, irregularity and disorder, Kames later insists, is painfully disagreeable and excites a sense of horror at its monstrosity (p. 450). But deviations are also monstrous in that they offer a lesson in what is not proper. When ruins are Gothic rather than classical they conform to an idea of enlightened progress. Indeed, Anna Barbauld's 'On Monastic Institutions' describes her 'secret triumph' at seeing the ruins of an old abbey. The ruins stand as testaments to the ascendancy of knowledge and reason and also, since they were of an old Catholic institution destroyed during the Reformation, Protestantism. 'Always consid-ered as the haunts of ignorance and superstition' by Barbauld, the ruins mark the ascendancy of neoclassical over Gothic values (p. 195).

RUINS, GRAVEYARDS AND THE POETRY OF THE PAST

Ruins and other forms of Gothic architecture assumed a different and positive significance in the course of the eighteenth century. The Gothic revival marked a major change in attitudes towards medieval styles. Though an increasing number of buildings in this style were commissioned, it was literary works that provided the impulse for the new taste. Antiquarianism, the vogue for the Graveyard school of poetry and intense interest in the sublime were significant features of the cultural environment that nurtured the Gothic revival. While the Gothic past continued to be constructed as the subordinated and distanced antithesis to Enlightenment culture, the events, settings, figures and images began to be considered on their own merits rather than as neoclassical examples of poor taste. Gothic style became the shadow that haunted neoclassical values, running parallel and counter to its ideas of symmetrical form, reason, knowledge and propriety.

Shadows, indeed, were among the foremost characteristics of Gothic works. They marked the limits necessary to the constitution of an enlightened world and delineated the limitations of neoclassical perceptions. Darkness, metaphorically, threatened the light of reason with what it did not know. Gloom cast perceptions of formal order and unified design into obscurity; its uncertainty generated both a sense of mystery and passions and emotions alien to reason. Night gave free reign to imagination's unnatural and marvellous creatures, while ruins testified to a temporality that exceeded rational understanding and human finitude. These were the thoughts conjured up by Graveyard poets.

Graveyard poetry was popular in the first half of the eighteenth century. Its principal poetic objects, other than graves and churchyards, were night, ruins, death and ghosts, everything, indeed, that was excluded by rational culture. It did not, however, idly or uncritically, celebrate them for its own sake. Robert Blair's 'The Grave' (1743) revels in images of death and encourages readers to think about the horrors of the grave, of night and ghosts not as a morbid fascination but rather as a warning to the godless. For Blair death is a 'gloomy path' (l. 687) that leads from earth to heaven. To contemplate death and its accompanying signs is to recognise the transience of physical things and pleasures: 'How shocking must thy Summons be, O *Death*! / To him that is at Ease in his possessions' (ll. 350–1). Death lays waste to material human aspirations:

> Soon, very soon, thy firmest Footing fails;
> And down dropp't into that darksome Place,
> Where *nor Device, nor knowledge* ever came.
>
> (ll. 294–6)

But it also elevates one's considerations to higher, spiritual objects and ends:

> Thrice welcome *Death*!
> That after many a painful bleeding Step
> Conducts us to our Home, and lands us safe
> On the long-wish'd for Shore.
>
> (ll. 706–9)

Death, as leveller of earthly desires and ambitions, demands religious faith and hope in order to pave the way for souls to ascend to heaven.

As a poem imbued with the sentiments of the Evangelical revival taking place in the eighteenth century, 'The Grave' enjoyed a long life in print as required reading for the spiritually-minded. Edward Young's *Night Thoughts* (1749–51) also received such acclaim. This much longer poem develops evangelical themes, but in a more extravagant fashion. In *Night Thoughts* the contemplation of death and decay serves to encourage speculations on the life to come. Fears of mortality and associated superstitions are unwarranted if one has faith. Confronting and overcoming the limits of material existence, *Night Thoughts* is organised by a play of images which double the significance of life and death, light and dark. For Young, the life of the body entombs the soul in darkness, while death and darkness enable the apprehension of a transcendent and immanent brilliance. It is for these reasons that night and darkness are so valued:

> *Darkness* has more Divinity for me,
> It strikes Thought inward, it drives back the Soul
> To settle on Herself, our Point supreme!
>
> (V, 128–30)

Darkness enables a person to perceive the soul within, it expands the mind by producing a consciousness of its own potential for divinity.

Although *Night Thoughts* alters the significance of Enlightenment metaphors of light and dark and goes beyond the limits of rationality and empirical knowledge in its efforts to inspire the individual imagination with a sense of religious mystery and wonder, its power as a moral text was beyond question. In many ways, the poem's warnings against corruption, depravity and atheism as well as many of its images of the Divinity, as a mighty mind, for instance, mark it out as a product of its age. Like other poems of its kind, *Night Thoughts* criticises ignorance and superstition. Thomas Parnell's 'Night-piece on Death' (1722), Nathaniel Cotton's 'Night-piece' (1751) and John Cunningham's 'The Contemplatist' (1762) all emphasise that the leveller, death, is not to be feared. Without fear the spectres and ghosts that haunt superstitious minds disappear. In the face of death, moreover, science remains impotent and blind. Graveyard poetry, its injunctions to nocturnal speculation on human finitude and the vanity of earthly ambitions, uses tombs, ruins, decay and ghosts as a mode of moral instruction rather than excitement.

The attractions of darkness, however, and the power of the images and visions it engendered were not lost on other poets associated with the melancholy evocations of the Graveyard school. William Collins's 'Ode to Fear' (1746) describes the fanciful and shadowy shapes, the monsters, giants and phantoms that the emotion produces. These figures testify less to the power of the grave in elevating thought to spiritual matters and more to the power of imagination:

> Dark power, with shuddering meek submitted thought,
> Be mine, to read the visions old,
> Which thy awakening bards have told.

(ll. 51–3)

Fear and the supernatural figures it conjures up is one of the 'divine emotions' that poets and bards of earlier ages were able to produce. To these the ode appeals for an imaginative power, a sense of nature and a capacity to evoke feelings unavailable in neoclassical compositions. The growing importance of older forms of writing are manifested in the lines from Joseph Warton's 'The Enthusiast' (1740): 'What are the lays of artful Addison, / Coldly correct, to Shakespear's warblings wild?' (ll. 166–7) Or, in the words of Joseph Warton's brother, Thomas, in his 'The Pleasures of Melancholy' (1745), 'But let the sacred genius of the night/ Such mystic visions send, as Spenser saw' (ll. 62–3).

Shakespeare and Spenser were considered to be the inheritors of a tradition of romantic writing that harked back to the Middle Ages. Like the songs of bards and minstrels, the emotional power of their descriptions of nature and visionary images were held up as examples of a more imaginative form of literary creation. Wildness of natural scenery, marvellous figures and lyrical style became signs of a re-evaluation of writing which privileged inventiveness and imagination over imitation and morality. 'The Pleasures of Melancholy', like many Graveyard poems, dwells on darkness, ghosts and tombs, but not in order to raise thoughts to heaven. The thoughts that it encourages are on the visionary and mystical power of writing, not to produce moral understanding, but to evoke intense feelings. This power, moreover, is linked, in the many images of storms, rocks and caverns to a dark and wild nature.

These departures from classical rules of imitation and creativity were supported by the work of antiquarians in their reassessments of old texts. Thomas Warton was himself a major figure in this process. His *History of English Poetry* (1774–81) traces the origins of romantic fiction to Arabia. From there it had started its migration across Europe during the period of the Crusades. Other scholars queried the idea of the Eastern origins of romances and preferred to identify the beginnings of romance among the Celtic, Saxon and Norse tribes of northern Europe. Of this opinion was Thomas Percy who, in his *Reliques of Ancient English Poetry* (1765), published a collection of romantic songs and ballads. Other collections, or in the case of Macpherson's *Ossian* poems (1762), fabrications, established the popularity of, as Percy's Dedication to the *Reliques* put it, 'the rude songs of ancient minstrels'. These 'barbarous productions of unpolished ages' were held up for approval 'not as the labours of art, but as the effusions of nature, showing the first efforts of ancient genius'. While the precise origins of romances remained a matter of scholarly dispute, their importance lay chiefly in the fact that they were not classical. Moreover, the recovery and validation of romances enabled certain neoclassical prejudices to be challenged. Thomas Warton wrote of how Gothic romances, though shaken by classical fictions, maintained their ground:

> the daring machineries of giants, dragons and enchanted castles, borrowed from the magic storehouse of Boiardo, Ariosto and Tasso, began to be employed by the epic muse. These ornaments have been censured by the bigotry of precise and servile critics, as abounding in whimsical absurdities, and as unwarrantable deviations from the practice of Homer and Virgil.

(IV, p. 360)

Such strong criticisms questioned the limits of neoclassical aesthetic values by developing, on the basis of romantic texts, different ideas about art, originality and nature.

In his *Letters on Chivalry and Romance* (1762), Richard Hurd is critical of the violence of neoclassical prejudices. The *Letters* argue that romances are derived from societies structured by chivalry and feudal customs. The argument, however, does not make its case with an analysis of medieval romances but focuses on writings that draw heavily upon them for their poetical effect. These writers, Hurd states, included Ariosto, Tasso, Spenser, Shakespeare and Milton, and

> were seduced by these barbarities of their forefathers; were even charmed by the Gothic Romances. Was this caprice and absurdity in them? Or, may there not be something in the Gothic Romance peculiarly suited to the views of a genius, and to the ends of poetry? And may not the philosophic moderns have gone too far, in their perpetual ridicule and contempt of it?
>
> (p. 4)

Invoking the acknowledged literary value associated with these writers, Hurd is able to defend the Gothic tradition against the extremes of eighteenth-century judgement. The Gothic influence is, moreover, bound up with the genius of these poets, making a significant contribution to the imaginative power of their poetry: Hurd contends that Spenser and Milton 'when most inflamed', poetically speaking, were 'more particularly rapt with the Gothic fables of chivalry' (p. 55).

The *Letters on Chivalry and Romance* not only challenge the prejudices of neoclassical criticism, they also begin a process of re-evaluation. Cultural productions, Hurd insists in an important displacement of neoclassical dominance, demand consideration on their own terms:

> When an architect examines a Gothic structure by Grecian rules, he finds nothing but deformity. But the Gothic architecture

> has its own rules, by which when it comes to be examined, it is
> seen to have its merit, as well as the Grecian.
>
> (p. 61)

Given the importance of classical forms of reason, knowledge,
imitation and morality in eighteenth-century judgements, Hurd
presents a major transformation of the function of criticism.
Hurd's *Letters*, however, do more than interrogate the homogeneity and consequent exclusiveness of neoclassical hierarchies
of taste: towards the end of the work these hierarchies undergo
a process of inversion. Hurd attacks, as a 'trite maxim' of bad
criticism, the view that poets must imitate nature. Poetical truth,
he argues, lies beyond the bounds of a natural order. Instead,
poetry should indulge imagination and range in marvellous,
magical and extraordinary worlds, worlds that are associated with
forms of nature that evoke a sense of wonder (pp. 91–4).

THE SUBLIME

Hurd's argument in favour of judging cultural productions
according to the rules employed in their composition, and his
case for a very different set of poetic values in which imagination
and genius come to the fore and nature becomes the source of
inspiration, can be aligned with changing attitudes to the relationship of art and nature. Natural scenery, for example, was being
perceived differently. Mountains, once considered as ugly blem-
ishes, deformities disfiguring the proportions of a world that
ideally should be uniform, flat and symmetrical, began to be seen
with eyes pleased by their irregularity, diversity and scale. The
pleasure arose from the range of intense and uplifting emotions
that mountainous scenery evoked in the viewer. Wonder, awe,
horror and joy were the emotions believed to expand or elevate the
soul and the imagination with a sense of power and infinity.
Mountains were the foremost objects of the natural sublime.

No topic of aesthetic enquiry in the eighteenth century

generated greater interest than the sublime. De Boileau's translation of Longinus on sublimity in the late seventeenth century inspired a host of writings examining the nature, objects and effects of the sublime, among the most influential of which was Edmund Burke's *A Philosophical Enquiry into the Origin of our Ideas of the Sublime and the Beautiful* (1757). For Burke, beautiful objects were characterised by their smallness, smoothness, delicacy and gradual variation. They evoked love and tenderness in contrast to the sublime which produced awe and terror. Objects which evoked sublime emotions were vast, magnificent and obscure. Loudness and sudden contrasts, like the play of light and dark in buildings, contributed to the sense of extension and infinity associated with the sublime. While beauty could be contained within the individual's gaze or comprehension, sublimity presented an excess that could not be processed by a rational mind. This excess, which confronted the individual subject with the thought of its own extinction, derived from emotions which, Burke argued, pertained to self-preservation and produced a *frisson* of delight and horror, tranquility and terror.

The terror was akin to the sense of wonderment and awe accompanying religious experience. Sublimity offered intimations of a great, if not divine, power. This power was experienced in many objects and not only in the grandeur of natural landscape. Gothic romances and poetry, which drew on the wildness and grandeur of nature for their inspiration, partook of the sublime. The awful obscurity of the settings of Graveyard poetry elevate the mind to ideas of wonder and divinity, while the similar settings of poems by Collins and the Wartons attribute a sacred, visionary and sublime power to the supernatural figures of ancient bards as well as to the wildness of nature. Hugh Blair, in his *Lectures on Rhetoric and Belles Lettres* (1783), identifies Gothic architecture as a source of the sublime: 'A Gothic cathedral raises ideas of grandeur in our minds, by its size, its height, its awful obscurity, its strength, its antiquity, and its durability' (p. 59). The irregularity, ornamentation, immensity of Gothic buildings overwhelmed the gaze with a vastness that suggested divinity and infinity. Age and durability were also features that evoked sublimity for an essayist writing 'On the Pleasure Arising from the Sight of Ruins or Ancient Structures' in the *European Magazine* (1795): 'No one of the least sentiment or imagination can look upon an old or ruined edifice without feeling sublime emotions; a thousand ideas croud upon his mind, and fill him with awful astonishment' (Monk, p. 141).

The interest in the sublime is crucial in the reappraisal of artefacts from the Gothic ages. Implicated in the transformation of ideas concerning nature and its relation to art, both Gothic and sublime objects also participated in a transformation of notions of individuality, in the mind's relation to itself as well as to natural, cultural and metaphysical worlds. John Baillie's *An Essay on the Sublime* (1747) gives a powerful account of what the sublime meant for an individual's sense of self:

> Hence comes the Name of *Sublime* to everything which thus raises the Mind to fits of *Greatness* and disposes it to soar above her *Mother Earth*; Hence arises that *Exultation* and *Pride* which the Mind ever feels from the *Consciousness* of its own *Vastness* – That *Object* only can be justly called *Sublime*, which in some degree disposes the Mind to this *Enlargement* of itself, and gives her a lofty *Conception* of her own *Powers*.
>
> (p. 4)

The vastness that had been glimpsed in the natural sublime became the mirror of the immensity of the human mind. Elevating and expanding mental powers to an almost divine extent signified the displacement of religious authority and mystery by the sublimity of nature and the human imagination. Sacred nature, glimpsed in sublime settings and evoked by old poetry and buildings, ceded to the genius and creative power of a sacred self. By means of natural and cultural objects of sublimity the human mind began its transcendence. In its imaginary ascendancy over nature, it discovered a grander scale and a new sense of power and freedom for itself.

This sense of freedom was neither purely subjective nor simply a matter of exceeding previous aesthetic forms. Freedom, in a political sense, was evoked in the process of recovering old texts, themselves markers of a history in which endured a different idea of nation and culture. It was a culture, if not entirely indigenous to Britain, that was distinguished from those of Greece or Rome and possessed of a history which had the permanence identified in Gothic architecture. Moreover, it was a culture believed to foster a love of liberty and democracy. Paul-Henri Mallett's Preface to his 1755 account of the early history of the Germanic tribes, translated by Percy as *Northern Antiquities* (1770), outlines these aspects of Gothic culture. It was among the nations of northern Europe and Scandinavia that European hatred of slavery and tyranny originated:

> is it not well known that the most flourishing and celebrated states of Europe owe originally to the northern nations, whatever liberty they now enjoy, either in their constitution, or in the spirit of their government? For although the Gothic form of government has been almost every where altered or abolished, have we not retained, in most things, the opinions, the customs, the manners which that government had a tendency to produce? Is not this, in fact, the principal source of that courage, of that aversion to slavery, of that empire of honour which characterize in general the European nations; and of that moderation, of that easiness of access, and peculiar attention to the rights of humanity, which so happily distinguish our sovereigns from the inaccessible and superb tyrants of Asia?
>
> (pp. 57–8)

Asia was not the only locus of tyranny. Closer to home was the tyranny that attended the decline of the Roman empire which became a site of despotism, degradation and barbarity and was itself overthrown by the Germanic tribes.

The significance of Gothic culture was cited in British political discussions from the mid-seventeenth century. Parliaments and the legal system, it was believed, were derived from Gothic institutions and peoples who were free and democratic. The word was employed loosely, embracing Celtic and Germanic tribes. The native culture that it referred to was one composed of those indigenous peoples and invaders whose occupation preceded the invasions of the Romans. Any relics of a non-Roman past were taken as evidence of a native and enduring tradition of independence. In 1739 one contributor to *Common Sense* wrote: 'Methinks there was something respectable in those old hospitable Gothick halls, hung round with the Helmets, Breast-plates, and Swords of our Ancestors; I entered them with a Constitutional Sort of Reverence and look'd upon those arms with Gratitude, as the Terror of former Ministers, and the Check of Kings' (Kliger, p. 27). Like the durability of Gothic buildings, these relics are reminders of the 'noble Strength and Simplicity' of the Gothic Constitution. The hierarchical relation of the meanings of 'Gothic' and 'Roman' was far less clear than eighteenth-century critics made out: privileged meanings of 'Gothic' or 'classical' alternated, polarised by the political positions of Whig or Tory that employed the terms.

The word 'Gothic' was thus implicated in an ongoing political struggle over meanings. In the mid-eighteenth century the tyranny of Rome signified more than a period in early European history. After the Reformation, Protestantism constructed Roman Catholicism as a breeding-ground of despotism and superstition. The resistance to the imposition of classical aesthetic values also vindicates an enduring idea of British national culture as both free, natural and imaginative. But 'Gothic' was also a term of abuse in other political positions. In the contest for the meaning of 'Gothic' more than a single word was at stake. At issue were the differently constructed and valued meanings of the Enlightenment, culture, nation and government as well as contingent, but no less contentious, significances of the family, nature, individuality and representation.

3

GOTHIC FORMS

Take – An old castle, half of it ruinous.
A long gallery, with a great many doors, some secret ones.
Three murdered bodies, quite fresh.
As many skeletons, in chests and presses . . .
Mix them together, in the form of three volumes, to be taken at any of the watering-places before going to bed.

(Anon., *Terrorist Novel Writing*, p. 229)

Other staple Gothic ingredients could be added to the recipe offered by an anonymous critic in an essay entitled 'Terrorist Novel Writing' (1797): dark subterranean vaults, decaying abbeys, gloomy forests, jagged mountains and wild scenery inhabited by bandits, persecuted heroines, orphans, and malevolent aristocrats. The atmosphere of gloom and mystery populated by threatening figures was designed to quicken readers' pulses in terrified expectation. Shocks, supernatural incidents and superstitious beliefs set out to promote a sense of sublime awe and wonder which entwined with fear and elevated imaginations. Though many devices and settings were repeated, they were inflected differently. A hybrid form from its inception, the Gothic blend of medieval and historical romance with the novel of life and manners was framed in supernatural, sentimental or sensational terms. The consistency of the genre relied on the settings, devices and events. While their project was the production of terror, their repeated use turned them into rather hackneyed conventions and then into objects of satire. Indeed, sublime aspirations often veered towards the ridiculous.

Detailing the absurdities, confusions and silly artifices of Gothic novels, satirical judgements regarded them negatively for their failure as representations of human life and manners and their lack of moral instruction. Like romances before them, Gothic novels were irrational, improper and immoral wastes of time. What was worse, however, was that they were popular as T. J. Matthias observes in *The Pursuits of Literature* (1796): 'The spirit of enquiry which he [Horace Walpole] introduced was rather frivolous, though pleasing, and his Otranto Ghosts have propagated their species with unequalled fecundity. The spawn is in every novel shop' (p. 422). Horace Walpole's *The Castle of Otranto* (1764) was recognised as the origin of this new, popular and prodigious species of writing.

Though it was the blueprint for a new mode of writing, the framework that was established by the *The Castle of Otranto* underwent a number of significant changes in the hands of later writers, under pressure from different historical circumstances. The relative consistency of Gothic settings and plots, however, in conjunction with the romance tradition from which it drew, enabled the Gothic novel to be recognisable as a distinct type of fiction and also exposed it to the attacks of literary satirists. Framed as another manifestation of the romance form or as a pastiche of the productions of uncivilised ages, Gothic novels could be readily criticised by the literary establishment. The tone, however, of the criticism became increasingly ambivalent: ridicule serves to reinforce social and literary values while simultaneously acknowledging some degree of anxiety. Indeed, the increasing popularity of the genre exacerbated the neoclassical fear that all romances and novels could produce antisocial effects and lead to social disintegration. Despite being associated with literary and moral impropriety, many Gothic novels set out to vindicate morality, virtue and reason. They were thus caught between their avowedly moral and conventional projects and the unacceptably unrealistic mode of representation they employed. This tension produced the ambivalence internal to the novels themselves as well as the critical reception they received. It also contributed to the subsequent changes in narrative strategy and setting.

While a certain ambivalence characterises both the structure of Gothic narratives and their relation to the literary codes of the time, it is an ambivalence that cannot be restricted to the sphere of literature itself. What literature was, its nature and function, was undergoing significant revision. This can be seen in the shifting attitude to non-classical texts, in the way 'Gothic' began to be positively associated with nature, feeling and the expansiveness of the individual imagination. Fiction was becoming less a mode of moral instruction, a guide to proper behaviour, a way of representing society as natural, unified and rational, and more an invitation to pleasure and excitement, a way of cultivating individual emotions detached from the obligations of the everyday world. While it freed the writer from neoclassical conventions, it also imaginarily liberated the reader from his or her place in society.

These changing attitudes to literature were part of wider shifts in the mode of literary production and consumption. Markets for and access to texts of all kinds were expanding as a result of cheaper printing processes and the emergence of circulating libraries. The growing reading public included larger numbers of readers from the middle class, especially women, and reflected a change in the distribution of power and wealth from an aristocratic and landed minority to those whose interests lay in a mercantile economy. Writing, too, was becoming less a pursuit associated with those who could afford leisure and more a professional activity. While this meant that individual writers were bound to sell their work, it also made them dependent on the market that consumed fiction. The popularity of the Gothic novel highlights the way that the control of literary production was shifting away from the guardians of taste and towards the reading public itself, much to the chagrin of those interested in maintaining an exclusive set of literary values. Women constituted an important part of this market, and not only as avid consumers of fiction. An increasing proportion of novels were written by women, often in order to maintain themselves and their families.

These shifts in the class and gender composition of readers are linked to social and political changes as well as economic ones. Industrialisation, urbanisation and the shifts of political power manifested in the American Revolution's rejection of imperialism (1776), and the French Revolution's overthrow of absolutist monarchy (1789), constitute the most general markers of changing notions of government, social organisation and individuality. All areas of British society were rendered unstable, as were its ways of representing and regulating itself according to rational and moral principles. While much Gothic fiction can be seen as a way of imagining an order based on divine or metaphysical principles that had been displaced by Enlightenment rationality, a way of conserving justice, privilege and familial and social hierarchies, its concern with modes of representing such an order required that it exceed the boundaries of reason and propriety. It is in this context that Gothic fiction can be said to blur rather than distinguish the boundaries that regulated social life, and interrogate, rather than restore, any imagined continuity between past and present, nature and culture, reason and passion, individuality and family and society.

THE CASTLE OF OTRANTO

Many of the main ingredients of the genre that was to be known as the Gothic novel can be found in Horace Walpole's *The Castle of Otranto*. While other novels, like Tobias Smollett's *The Adventures of Ferdinand Count Fathom* (1753), used feudal customs and settings or characters, it was Walpole's text that condensed features from old poetry, drama and romance and provided the model for future developments. In the preface to the second edition of *The Castle of Otranto*, Horace Walpole both situated the novel in relation to romances and novels and justified its project in terms of the move away from neoclassical aesthetic values. The novel, he states, 'was an attempt to blend the two kinds of romance, the antient and the modern' (p. 7). The mixing of medieval romance and realistic novel tries to overcome the perceived limitations of both: the latter's insistence on realistic representation of nature and life cramps the imagination while the former is too unnatural and improbable. Wanting to let fancy roam freely in 'the boundless realms of invention' and create 'more interesting situations', Walpole also states his intention to preserve rules of probability and have his characters 'think, speak and act, as it might be supposed mere men and women would do in extraordinary positions'. The story, however, inclines more to the presentation of marvellous events than to human characterisation and realistic action.

In the second preface Walpole appeals to new ideas about writing. Inspiration, individual artistic genius and imaginative freedom overstep the boundaries of neoclassical taste. The originality and genius of Shakespeare legitimates imaginative licence as well as being cited as a major influence on the novel's dramatic, even melodramatic, contrasts of figures, its pace, dialogue and the effects of its setting and its use of supernatural events. Despite these justifications for this 'new species of romance', the preface maintains a certain distance, aware of its transgression of certain aesthetic norms. Written in the third person, the preface, though acknowledging authorship, tries to negotiate a compromise as well as distance the writer from any impropriety that might be detected. Novels and romances were far from being completely acceptable pastimes for a member of polite society. Indeed, it was only the success of the first edition of the novel, published anonymously, that led to Walpole's admission of authorship.

For the development of the Gothic novel, the significance of anonymous publication is more than the recognition of impropriety associated with authorial disavowal. The first edition had a preface that became a crucial device in Gothic narratives: it was itself a fiction, a fiction, moreover, with pretensions to historical authenticity and veracity. The antiquarian tones of the preface declare *The Castle of Otranto* to be a translation of a medieval Italian story printed in 1529 and written at the time of the Crusades. Everything, from the Gothic script in which it is printed to the feudal customs and miraculous incidents it presents, conspires to give it an air of truth as a production of the barbarous and superstitious dark ages. Its moral, questionable to the eighteenth-century 'translator' – that 'the sins of the fathers are visited on their children' – also establishes a foundation for later stories. Doubting whether 'ambition curbed its appetite of dominion from the dread of so remote a punishment', the 'translator' judges an avowedly superstitious past in the terms of his present. The historical distance that is opened up by the device of the discovered manuscript returns readers to the neoclassical strictures and produces an uncomfortable interplay between past and present that both displaces and confronts contemporary aesthetic and social concerns. Historical distance also acknowledges cultural difference: English Protestant culture is distinguished from the southern European, and thus Catholic, background which is constructed as both exotic and superstitious, fascinating but extreme in its aesthetic and religious sentiments.

The Castle of Otranto tells the story of Manfred, prince of

Otranto by virtue of his grandfather's usurpation of the rightful owner, and his attempts to secure his lineage. His sickly son is crushed by a gigantic helmet on the day of his wedding to Isabella, daughter of another noble. The helmet comes from the statue of the original owner and, despite the physical impossibility, the credulous followers of Manfred blame and imprison a young peasant, Theodore, for its miraculous transportation. Ambitious and unscrupulous as he is, Manfred decides that, though already married, he will have to wed Isabella in order to produce an heir. Repulsed at his advances, Isabella is saved by the sighing portrait of Manfred's grandfather. She flees from the castle, helped by a recently escaped Theodore, through subterranean vaults. The youth, however, is recaptured. At the same time, servants are terrified by the sight of a giant in armour and Manfred, jealous of an imagined attachment between Theodore and Isabella, threatens his life. A friar, Jerome, intercedes, and discovers the youth to be his long-lost son.

A troop of knights arrive at the castle carrying a gigantic sword (which matches the helmet) and the colours of Isabella's family. Suspicious of Manfred, the knights join the search for her. In the meantime, Theodore is helped to escape by Mathilda, Manfred's rejected daughter, and flees through the castle vaults to encounter Isabella among a labyrinth of caverns. There, to defend her honour, he defeats a knight in combat and discovers him to be Isabella's father, Frederic. Back at the castle, the conjugal problems are still unresolved. Theodore is attracted by Mathilda, as is Frederic. At the mention of this amorous interest, blood runs from the nose of Alphonso's statue. Manfred, finding the lovers in the chapel and believing Mathilda to be Isabella, stabs her in a fit of passion. His guilt and his forebears' guilt is discovered, Jerome and Theodore are revealed to be the true heirs to Otranto and, with a clap of thunder and a clanking of ghostly chains, the castle crumbles to ruin. The guilty die or incarcerate themselves in convents and proper lineage is restored with a warning about human vanities and with the eventual marriage of Theodore and Isabella.

While *The Castle of Otranto* sets out the features and themes for use in all later Gothic texts, it does so in a rather ambivalent way. The aristocratic order of primogeniture, property and patriarchy that it restores with such speed, and so many convolutions, stretches the bounds of credulity and reduces the basis of feudal society to a few of the more extravagant customs. Even as it associates virtue and character with breeding (Theodore is never anything but a knight in peasant's clothes) and seems to naturalise patriarchal and aristocratic values within a wider metaphysical order governed by supernatural manifestations of an eternal law, its mode of representation undercuts these links. For the supernatural manifestations of the restitution of an old order present a law that is at once violent and sublime, disproportionate and just, and founded as much on superstition as on power. Despite the comedy of the servants' superstitious fears, superstition is encouraged by the irrational and anti-Enlightenment manifestation of gigantic and supernatural justice.

Indeed, the novel's style stimulates emotional effects rather than rational understanding, thereby emulating the vicious passions of the selfish and ambitious villain. The frenetic pace of the text is, in part, an effect of excitement and irrationality. In a letter to the Reverend William Cole (9 March 1765), Walpole describes how his own Gothic mansion and its decorations contributed to the dream he offers as the origin of the story. These factors centre the interest of the story on marvellous and threatening events and the terrors they produce instead of moral resolution. The style of writing itself works against reason and propriety and led critics of the time to baulk at its absurdities, lack of morality and false taste. The story's pretence to historical veracity exposed the artifice of its representations for an audience judging by neoclassical standards. Its extravagant depictions of passions and incredible events and the thinness of its cautionary ending leaves, as the 'translator' notes in the first preface, an eighteenth-century reader suspicious of its supposed morality. But its contrast of distinct aesthetic impulses leaves the text itself in an uncertain position between offering a serious purpose or a subversive play. Its evocations of terror and superstition can be seen to advocate a sense of awe at supernatural power and its restitution of justice, or can render such a notion of justice comic and suggest that the orders which depend on such superstitious notions are quaintly unrealistic. If ideals of chivalrous virtue and honour depend on spectral appearances and supernatural wrath to preserve them then they, like the castle itself, may be destined for ruin. Chivalry and honour, indeed, are like ghostly incarnations of an old order that have no place in the enlightened eighteenth century. Mere superstitions, these ideals, while underpinning aristocratic and patriarchal culture, have no power against the cunning and tyranny of the selfish and ambitious individual. Virtue, too, is helpless in the face of tyrannical fathers interested only in the preservation of a law of primogeniture. Confronted with indifference, forced marriage and death, their lot, it seems, is to suffer and be sacrificed to the persecutions of patriarchal power with only the occasional knight fighting for their honour. Indeed, the predominance of arms and armour presents a culture founded on a violence that is constructed as both metaphysical and individual. But it is not, in eighteenth-century terms, natural.

In this respect, *The Castle of Oranto* can be seen as a reinforcement of eighteenth-century values, distinguishing the barbaric past from the enlightened present. None the less, eighteenth-century culture still depended on notions of virtue and honour. Nor did it witness the total disappearance of an aristocratic order, of which Walpole, later to become Earl of Orford, was a part. From the position offered by the second preface, however, with its advocation of imagination and original genius and its privileging of individualist values, the novel appears as a text that examines the limitations of reason, virtue and honour in the regulation of the passions, ambitions and violence underlying patriarchal and family orders. Despite their significant interrelation, distinctions between terms and values are left unresolved. *The Castle of Otranto* displays the tensions and contradictions traversing eighteenth-century society's representations of itself. It was ambivalently received by reviewers in the 1760s. For one, not knowing whether the translator 'speaks seriously or ironically', the absurdity of its contents and wretchedness of its conclusion were not sufficiently compensated for by the 'well marked' characters and the 'spirit and propriety of the narrative'. For another, the Gothic machinery is entertaining, the language is accurate and its representations of character, manners and humanity 'indicate the keenest penetration'. Its 'principal defect', however, is its lack of any moral but the 'very useless' one concerning the sins of the father. In contrast to reviews that noticed, and approved of, eighteenth-century shapings of character, another reviewer criticised 'the foibles of a supposed antiquity' and went on to declare that 'it is, indeed, more than strange, that an Author, of a refined and polished genius, should be an advocate for re-establishing the barbarous superstitions of Gothic devilism!' (McNutt, pp. 163–4).

The ambivalent reactions produced by *The Castle of Otranto* partake of a wider ambivalence concerning the eighteenth century's relation to its Gothic past and its changing present. The function of literature in representing a rational and natural social order and guiding readers in proper modes of conduct and discrimination is also questioned: in failing to offer an overriding and convincing position, *The Castle of Otranto* leaves readers unsure of its moral purpose. Its uncertain tone and style, between seriousness and irony, is perhaps the novel's cardinal sin and one that is visited in various forms on all its literary offspring. Rending the homogenising correspondence of representation and reality, Gothic fancy and invention was able to construct other worlds that dislocated boundaries between fact and fiction, history and contemporaneity, reality and fantasy. The loosening of rational and moral rules for writing facilitated by the idea of the individual imagination, and the indulgence of emotions and pleasures, also entailed evocations of anxiety – evinced by figures of darkness and power – that any form of justice or order, whether natural, human or supernatural, had itself become spectral.

EARLY REVISIONS

Walpole's excessive use of supernatural and irrational impulses, however, was tempered in subsequent Gothic works. In 1777 *The Champion of Virtue. A Gothic Story* was published anonymously in the guise of a translated old manuscript. This device itself acknowledges the influence of *The Castle of Otranto*. In 1778 the preface to the second edition, in which Clara Reeve declared her authorship and changed the title to *The Old English Baron*, outlined criticisms of Walpole's text. Its ability to engage the reader's sympathy is praised but 'the machinery is so violent, that it destroys the effect it is intended to excite' (p. 4). As a result the novel exceeds the limits of probability and credibility, disappointing instead of interesting readers: 'when your expectation is wound up to the highest pitch, these circumstances take it down with a witness, destroy the work of the imagination, and instead of attention, excite laughter' (p. 5). In the light of these criticisms *The Old English Baron* attempts to reduce the ambivalent effects of Gothic fiction, and restore a balance between marvellous and supernatural incident and the natural life and manners of eighteenth-century realism.

Ghostly machinations are kept to a minimum and, though the customs and settings of feudal times are invoked, they are contained by eighteenth-century sentiments. One contemporary critic observed that the book's claim to Gothic status arose primarily from the architectural descriptions (McNutt, p. 171). Although other critics gave relatively favourable reviews of the novel, Walpole was less than impressed by its claims to be a Gothic story:

'Have you seen "The Old English Baron", he wrote in a letter to Reverend William Mason (8 April 1778), 'a Gothic story, professedly written in imitation of Otranto, but reduced to reason and probability? It is so probable that any trial for murder at the Old Bailey would make a more interesting story!' (*Old English Baron*, Introduction, 1977, p. viii). For Walpole, Reeve's text elided the excitements of a very different past by framing it in the terms of a neoclassical present. *The Old English Baron* establishes a historical continuity maintained by the imposition of eighteenth-century rules and morality. Differences between Walpole and Reeve, moreover, implied disagreements that were not solely concerned with the purpose and place of literature. Unlike the aristocrat, Walpole, Reeve came from an educated middle-class background, her father being a curate in Ipswich. This social position is reflected in the novel's highlighting of gentility and merit, dissociated from social position. The hero's virtues, for instance, are not solely related to his high birth, since he was raised by a peasant family. His courage, kindness and generosity of spirit qualify him as one deserving of his advantages rather than merely inheriting them. Gothic devices and setting are subordinated to the social and domestic proprieties of the emerging middle class of the eighteenth century.

Set during the reign of Henry VI, the novel tells the story of a foundling, Edmund, of ostensibly peasant birth, who distinguishes himself in social and military skills. He is steward to the sons of Baron Fitz-Owen whose family inhabit a castle owned by a relation, Lord Lovel. The castle has a decayed set of apartments that have been mysteriously locked for years. Edmund's past is linked to these apartments. After his talents have excited rivalries in the Baron's family, he is sent to the apartments to spend the night. There, groans and strange lights lead to a dream in which he sees a knight in armour and a lady who address him as their child. Consequently, Edmund attempts to discover the truth of his parentage, gathered from diverse local anecdotes. After a feudal combat, the sins of Lord Lovel are brought to light and Edmund is established as the rightful heir to the castle and estates. Propriety as well as property is restored. The usurper is punished and Edmund is allowed to marry the Baron's daughter, thus harmonising family relations. Morality, too, is restored: 'All these, when together, furnish a striking lesson to posterity, of the over-ruling hand of Providence, and the certainty of RETRIBUTION' (p. 153). Not only do virtue, morality and social and domestic harmony prevail, they are, so the cautionary ending declares, divinely sanctioned and protected.

Though it reduces the incidence and effects of supernatural powers, the story none the less invokes heavenly might as a guarantee of the tale's moral. While its subjects are aristocratic and its world is feudal, the story keeps superstition in check with its emphasis on virtuous character, individual merit, human vanities and domestic order. Returned to a distinctly eighteenth-century framework, the fiction absorbs and rewrites the past in a manner which privileges the neoclassical present. In this respect, the relationship between history and fiction highlighted by Gothic tales is more complicated than the novel's preface acknowledges: 'history represents human nature as it is in real life; . . . romance displays only the amiable side of the picture' (p. 3). Unlike Walpole's version of a wild and irrational feudal past, Reeve's romance renders history itself as an amiable picture of eighteenth-century nature and life which in turn discloses them as somewhat unreal. Disturbing the boundaries between past and present, however, became an inevitable feature of Gothic fiction, even though the manner in which the two were articulated differed from writer to writer. History, like nature, the supernatural and the passions of individuals, became a contradictory site for both imaginative speculation and moral imposition.

In Sophia Lee's *The Recess* (1783–5) the interweaving of history and Gothic romance is complicated further. The novel situates its fictional heroines in a world populated by real figures and events from the Elizabethan age. Sir Philip Sidney, Sir Francis Drake and the Earl of Leicester as well as Elizabeth I all contribute to the plot. Spicing fiction with fact, however, did not lend the tale greater veracity. For one critic it detracted from the narrative. History was employed 'too lavishly', leaving the mind 'ever divided and distracted when the fact so little accords with the fiction, and Romance and History are at perpetual variance with one another' (*The Recess*, Introduction, p. xxiii). Romance, however, to use Reeve's distinction, does not win out in painting the real life of history in an amiable light. For several critics the novel's melancholic and gloomy tones were at odds with the romance form. Historical accuracy, indeed, is not a primary concern of the novel in which fictional licence freely alters events and their chronology. In many ways it serves as the backdrop for the representation of eighteenth-century concerns. Critics noted the novel's 'neglect of the peculiar manners of the age' while appreciating it as an instructive and interesting text (Introduction, pp. xxi–xxii). Gothic elements feature as part of the wider plot of a historical narrative that owes much to the extravagant composition of seventeenth-century French romances. Ruins, underground vaults and heroines' terrified flights are blended with romantic adventures ranging over a wide geographical area. Picturesque descriptions of natural scenery and accounts of domestic happiness, sufferings and tensions, however, maintain a thoroughly eighteenth-century perspective.

The use of history in *The Recess* introduced some important new directions for the Gothic model derived from Walpole. Like Reeve, it reduced the incidence of the supernatural and also gave new impetus to the historical romance, a form in which past events are liberally recomposed in fictional narrative. Unlike both Reeve and Walpole, however, the action of the novel centres on the lives of two women. They are the daughters of Mary Queen of Scots who have to be hidden from society and the court of Elizabeth in order not to suffer the same fate as their mother. They grow up in secret in the subterranean chambers of a ruined abbey. The novel charts their entry into the world under assumed names and their marriages to Lord Leicester and the Earl of Essex. Society and marriage offer only brief moments of happiness until the secret of their identity is disclosed. The disclosure leads to the death of one sister and the flight of the other, powerless against the political intrigues and violent passions of the Elizabethan world.

The world at large presents the greatest terrors for the young heroines. Rather than the imaginary threats of supernatural powers it is the accounts of pursuit and persecution by noblemen, female courtiers and hired bandits that constitute the major instances of fear. In contrast, domesticity, represented by the sentimental attachments of the sisters in their hidden, underground habitation, offers love and security. However, the novel suggests that there is no refuge in secrecy, hidden recesses or domesticity itself. The outside world invades the private, domestic sphere, turning a refuge into a place of dark menace. In its focus on female virtue, *The Recess* seems to take a pessimistic position in regard to its primary location in domestic space. Virtuous women continually confront suffering and persecution, their ideals leaving them both powerless and unrewarded. Neither virtue nor the security of domestic space forms an adequate defence and itself becomes a prison rather than a refuge, a restricted space confined by a system of values that privileges the male and active world beyond the family. At the same time romances marked a putative and contradictory attempt to offer access to worlds other than the domestic and family spheres that constituted the real life and manners of the majority of middle-class women. At home they could read tales that, while reinforcing ideals of female virtue and propriety, offered some escape from domestic confinement through fictional adventures even if, in the fictions, the impulse came from external violence. Foregrounding confinement, virtue in suffering, and a threatening external world, fiction none the less attempted to articulate the contradictory requirements of propriety and excitement. The resulting ambivalence only entwines the realms of women's reality and fantasy. The novel, by a successful writer and headmistress of a girls' school in Bath, is traversed by these contradictory impulses: the moral and social imperative to inculcate female virtues and domestic values conflicts with the fact that working in the world involves some transgression of the accepted position and role for women. In its highlighting of problems in ideals of female virtue and domesticity *The Recess* establishes an important direction for the Gothic novel.

Neither virtue nor propriety were a particular concern of William Beckford's *Vathek*, published in French in 1782 and translated into English in 1786. Frequently cited as a Gothic novel, *Vathek* remains distinct from the genre, though its influence can be traced in later and more obviously Gothic texts. One of the main connections is that its author, the extremely wealthy Beckford, built an extravagant and costly Gothic building, Fonthill Abbey. Like Walpole and his Gothic mansion at Strawberry Hill, he thought of the intricate and sublime architecture of Fonthill as a source of inspiration for his novel, comparing it to the hall of Eblis in *Vathek*. There are many evocations of sublimity in the natural and supernatural descriptions of the novel. The hero-villain, Caliph Vathek, is an Eastern tyrant whose violent actions and passionate temper can inspire terror and horror among his subjects. Vathek is also a sensualist, building great palaces in order to indulge his carnal pleasures. Adept in the arts of astrology and magic, the Caliph fervently pursues forbidden knowledge, until he is finally damned.

Though many antiquarians believed that the romance tradition originated in Arab or Eastern countries, *Vathek* is part of a different tradition of eighteenth-century writing. Translations of Arabian stories led to a vogue for Oriental tales and a love of the exotic. The East constituted another space in which the expanding imagination could freely roam. Indulgence in descriptions of excessive passion, irrational violence, magical events and sensual pleasure was acceptable, as many critics of *Vathek* seemed to agree, because they demonstrated the disastrous consequences of those forms of behaviour. *Vathek*'s ending aligns itself with this code: describing how Vathek will wander eternity in anguish, the concluding moral declares that 'such was, and should be, the punishment of unrestrained passions and atrocious deeds!' (p. 120). Ironically, and perhaps as a satire on eighteenth-century orientalism, this warning against excess comes at the end of a story that has flagrantly indulged in imaginative and descriptive excess.

The ending, like the uncomfortable identification with the hero-villain throughout the tale, refuses to affirm in the manner of romances any stable boundary line between good and evil. Vathek is the villain and also the victim of his ambitions and passions. Like Faust, having overvaulted his quest for knowledge and power, he incurs damnation at the hands of a violent super-natural order. The moral tone of the ending, as in *The Castle of Otranto*, remains unconvincing. Like Walpole's novel, *Vathek* makes no concessions to reason or probability, indulging in the imaginative pleasures of supernatural and fantastic events for the sublime emotions they produce rather than the morals they present.

In the connections and contrasts manifested in the writings of Walpole and Beckford, on the one hand, and Reeve and Lee on the other, two of the major strands of Gothic fiction are displayed. Despite differences of historical and geographical setting, the male writers of Gothic, of a more aristocratic class position, lean towards representations of irrationality and the supernatural, exercising the privileges and freedoms conferred by gender and class position. The female writers, usually more solidly middle-class in origin, remain more concerned with the limits of eighteenth-century virtues, careful to interrogate rather than overstep the boundaries of domestic propriety which, because of their gender, were more critically maintained. Though darkness, ruin, superstition and human passion are objects of fascination and sublimity in both strains, their significance and effect is shaped by the very different ends of the narratives. The Gothic fictions that dominated the 1790s introduced certain changes into the genre but the basic pattern of the narratives, as well as the conventional settings, can be directly identified with these two strategies of indulging or rationalising imaginative excess.

4

GOTHIC WRITING IN THE 1790s

Perhaps at this point we ought to analyze these new novels in which sorcery and phantasmagoria constitute practically the entire merit: foremost among them I would place *The Monk*, which is superior in all respects to the strange flights of Mrs Radcliffe's brilliant imagination. But this would take us too far afield. Let us concur that this kind of fiction, whatever one may think of it, is assuredly not without merit: 'twas the inevitable result of the revolutionary shocks which all Europe has suffered.

(Marquis de Sade, 'Reflections on the Novel', pp. 108–9)

The 1790s can be called the decade of Gothic fiction. It was the period when the greatest number of Gothic works were produced and consumed. Terror was the order of the day. Gothic stories littered literary magazines, three- and four-volume novels filled the shelves of circulating libraries and, in their cheap card covers, found their way into servants' quarters as well as drawing rooms. Though the startling Gothic machinery of *The Castle of Otranto* was set to work in every text, there were significant shifts in emphasis. These tended to follow the lines laid down by Reeve and

Lee in their framing of the past in terms of a rational and moral present. Eighteenth-century values were never far from the surface in these tales of other times. Terror, moreover, had an over-whelming political significance in the period. The decade of the French Revolution saw the most violent of challenges to monar-chical order. In Britain the Revolution and the political radicalism it inspired were represented as a tide of destruction threatening the complete dissolution of the social order. In Gothic images of violence and excessive passion, in villainous threats to proper domestic structures, there is a significant overlap in literary and political metaphors of fear and anxiety: metaphors that imply how much a culture, like the heroine and the family, sensed itself to be under attack both from within, in the dissemination of radical ideas, and from without, in the shape of revolutionary mobs across the Channel.

ANN RADCLIFFE

The most successful of Gothic writers was undoubtedly Ann Radcliffe, a woman whose uneventful life in many ways mirrored that of her middle-class audience. Married to a lawyer who became editor of a literary magazine, she appears to have spent most of her time at their home in Bath. Her novels were enormously popular and also received critical approbation. An index of her popularity can be seen in the amounts she was paid by booksellers: *The Mysteries of Udolpho* (1794) and *The Italian* (1797) earned her the then huge sums of £500 and £600. Radcliffe's popularity is also attested to by the many imitators of her work. Well into the nineteenth century books were produced using her narrative techniques, and even parts of her titles. Like Sophia Lee, Radcliffe chose virtuous young women as heroines of novels set in the Middle Ages or the Renaissance. Like Walpole, her geographical settings were usually in southern European countries, Italy and France in particular, continuing the association of Catholicism with superstition, arbitrary power and passionate extremes. The physical settings, too, were suitably Gothic: isolated and ruined castles and abbeys, old chateaux with secret vaults and passageways, dark forests and spectacular mountain regions populated by bandits and robbers. Radcliffe's heroines suffer repeated pursuit and incarceration at the hands of malevolent and ambitious aristocrats and monks. Orphans separated from protective domestic structures, these heroines journey through a mysteriously threatening world composed of an unholy mixture of social corruption, natural decay and imagined supernatural power. At the end virtue has, of course, been preserved and domestic harmony has been reaffirmed. The tales are all framed as lessons in virtue and faith in a guiding providential hand.

Where Radcliffe's tales differ significantly from previous Gothic texts is in their production and development of terrifying scenes and mysterious occurrences. In response to the strange noises and spectral figures that inhabit the dark world of ruins, castles and forests, the heroines conjure up images of ghostly supernatural forces. Imagined supernatural terrors are accompanied by other mysteries that lie closer to home and reality. *A Sicilian Romance* (1790) describes the mysterious hauntings in locked apartments and unravels the family secrets that underlie them. In *The Romance of the Forest* (1791) the heroine discovers an old manuscript that, to her horror, tells the story of a murdered man. In *The Mysteries of Udolpho* a brief glimpse of her father's letters leaves the heroine to speculate on the horrible secret, a concealed crime, buried in her family history. Family secrets are resolved and often rendered innocent, but only after a series of repeated invocations have encouraged heroine and reader alike to imagine the darkest possible outcome. Apparently spectral events are similarly explained after they have excited curiosity and terror over extended sections of the narrative. This use of suspense characterises Radcliffe's technique. Involving readers, like the heroines, in the narrative, the use of suspense encourages imaginations to indulge in extravagant speculations. The rational explanations that are subsequently offered, however, undercut the supernatural and terrible expectations and bring readers and characters back to eighteenth-century conventions of realism, reason and morality by highlighting their excessive credulity. While extremes of imagination and feeling are described in the novels, the object is always to moderate them with a sense of propriety.

Radcliffe's heroines come from the sentimental genre of fiction in which fine feelings are signs of virtue and nobility. They have a tendency, however, to overindulge their emotions, partaking too heavily of the cult of sensibility which flowered in the eighteenth century. Rarefied abandonments to feeling leave heroes and heroines in tears at the slightest melancholy thought and fainting at the smallest shock. Like the extravagant and superstitious imaginings that are displayed throughout Radcliffe's works, excessive sensibility is shown in order to indicate its dangerous evocation of passions that corrupt the heart. Powerful feelings are legitimately expressed in the responses to the magnificence of the scenery through which heroines pass. Radcliffe draws upon eighteenth-century notions of the picturesque and the sublime as well as the work of travel writers and painters. Elevated by undulating rural landscapes and awed by the craggy grandeur of the Alps and Appenines, the responses of Radcliffe's heroines are thoroughly in tune with prevailing aesthetic taste, and particularly well versed in Burkean ideas of the sublime and the beautiful. Such taste is reinforced with quotations of poetry from, or in the style of, the works of writers associated with the imaginative genius and natural sublimity of the Gothic age. Invoking poetic power, Radcliffe's texts also set out to contain it within orders of reason, morality and domesticity.

The most famous and most imitated of Radcliffe's six novels was *The Mysteries of Udolpho*. Its four volumes tell the story of Emily St Aubert. Brought up in a rural chateau in southern France by a caring father, Emily is educated in the virtues of simplicity and domestic harmony. She is prone, however, to overindulge her sensibilities. Her father, before he dies, warns her that all excess is vicious, especially excessive sensibility. Taken in by her aunt, Emily almost marries Valancourt, a similarly sentimental young nobleman. Instead, her aunt marries the Marquis Montoni and takes Emily to Venice and thence to the castle of Udolpho. Montoni is the dark villain of the story who tries by menacing and murderous means to secure Emily's estates. She flees from his persecution and the imagined terrors of the castle by way of the mouldering vaults of a ruined Gothic chapel. Later, supposedly supernatural terrors are explained, as is the very worldly identity of Montoni: he is leader of a group of banditti, not a demon. Emily returns to France and to the security of an aristocratic family who live in the region in which she was born. Despite the return to the simplicity of country life, fears of ghostly machinations propel the narrative, until an exhaustive series of explanations unravels both the mysteries of the castle and those disturbing secrets closer to home. With the return of Valancourt, absent from most of the narrative as a result of falling prey to the charms of a Countess and the corruptions of society, domestic happiness is restored. The novel announces its moral: that the power of vice is as temporary as its punishment is certain and that innocence, supported by patience, always triumphs in the end.

With a clear moral concluding the tale, Radcliffe, like Reeve, gives Gothic fiction a more acceptable face. Critics were generally pleased by Radcliffe's novels. *The Mysteries of Udolpho* was praised for its correctness of sentiment, its elegance of style and its bold and proper characterisation in the *Monthly Review* (1794). The author's imaginative and descriptive powers were admired by reviewers in the *European Magazine* (1794) and the *British Critic* (1794). Aspects of her style, however, provoked a degree of critical ambivalence. Her technique of prolonging the mysteries through her use of suspense was considered excessive. In the *Critical Review* (1794), Coleridge argued that 'curiosity is raised oftener than it is gratified; or rather, it is raised so high that no adequate gratification can be given it' (p. 362). A similar air of disappointment is evident in the critic in the *Gentleman's Magazine* (1794) who found the depictions of the picturesque repetitious. Another reviewer, in the *British Critic* (1794), stated that 'the lady's talent for description leads her to excess', before observing that 'too much of the terrific' leads to jaded sensibility and exhausted curiosity (pp. 120–1). These criticisms of the novel's excess point to a contradiction between the style and project of the novel which was to warn against the dangers of excess. Ironically, the criticisms also offer some insight into the ambiguous nature of Radcliffe's technique of suspense and deflating explanation. Like the writer of the satirical essay, 'Terrorist Novel Writing', who hopes that so many tales of ghosts and terror will satiate the most ravenous of reading publics with repetitions, *Udolpho*'s concern with the dangers of over-indulging sensibility and imagination involves the exaggeration of terrifying incidents in order to jade sensibility and exhaust superstitious curiosity. Readers are thus enlisted in the narrative as dupes of the false and terrifying expectations it sets up and then distanced from the credulities and superstitions of heroines and servants by the disappointing explanations. By the end, virtue, reason and domestic felicity are restored along with a discriminating readership.

None the less, the ambiguity of this technique of inviting and depicting the superstitions that it disavows produces ambivalent effects. The novel as a whole depends on the play of antitheses. It is only in contrast to the dark world of Udolpho that a world of happiness and light can be valued. Only by encountering the effects of excessive sensibility and imagination can Emily learn the virtue of moderation. In the passions and selfishness of the unscrupulous Montoni are manifested the terrifying effects of a loss of virtue and self-control. Against the rural simplicity and domestic happiness of the family home stands a threatening image of the social world as a place of artifice, corruption and violence. In Udolpho's world of imagination and terror one glimpses the face of evil. This face is as much that of the castle as the villain himself: 'Silent, lonely and sublime, it seemed to stand the sovereign of the scene, and to frown defiance on all, who dared to invade its solitary reign' (p. 227). The castle appears as a figure of power, tyranny and malevolence. Linked to Montoni it is a symbol of egoism, but it is in the imaginative eyes of Emily that it becomes awful.

Evil, focused in the castle itself, is a result of both the individual passions that are engendered by social corruption and the excessive sensibility that gives it supernatural power. The articulation of these two strands of vicious excess, vicious precisely because they lead away from the simplicity of reason and morality, is made possible by the excesses of the narrative: its artificial stimulation of terrors allow readers, like heroines, to imagine such power. In this way *Udolpho* is concerned with the effects of representation and the way that it can discriminate between, or blur, the boundaries of good and evil.

Towards the end of the third volume of the novel an exchange takes place that manifests a degree of self-consciousness about Gothic novels themselves. Its self-consciousness and satirical edge, indeed, prefigure the exchange about 'horrid' novels between Henry Tilney and Catherine Morland in Jane Austen's satire of the novel in *Northanger Abbey* (1818):

> 'Where have you been so long?' said she, 'I had begun to think some wonderful adventure had befallen you, and that the giant of this enchanted castle, or the ghost, which, no doubt, haunts it, had conveyed you through a trap-door into some sub-terranean vault, whence you was never to return.' 'No', replied Blanche, laughingly, 'you seem to love adventures so well, that I leave them for you to achieve.'
> 'Well, I am willing to achieve them, provided I am allowed to describe them.'
> 'My dear Mademoiselle Bearn,' said Henri, as he met her at the

door of the parlour, 'no ghost of these days would be so savage as to impose silence on you. Our ghosts are more civilized
than to condemn a lady to a purgatory severer even, than their
own, be it what it may.'

(p. 473)

The satirical dismissal of ghosts indicates the proper attitude
towards the supernatural: it is no more than the effects of a silly,
overindulged imagination associated with women of lower class.
In the context of the novel, however, the distancing of ghosts from
its present is a little more complicated. It is among this family
that Emily arrives after escaping the terrors of Udolpho. The two
female speakers participating in the discussion of ghosts from the
security of their domestic position, as aristocratic daughters or
family retainers, constitute doubles of Emily: one is rational, the
other overindulged in imagination and sensibility. These two,
indeed, represent the extreme positions allocated for the reader
by the novel.

But the secure world of the de Villefort family is not so neatly
divided nor so clearly distinguished from Udolpho's world of
terrors. The world of the de Villeforts is also populated by ghosts,
suggestively animated by strange noises and spectral figures
conveyed along subterranean passages. It is, moreover, the place
where the terrors of Udolpho catch up with Emily and are only
later explained. Other ghosts, emanating from a source that
is closer to home, are raised up. In the rural retreat of the de
Villeforts the horror that Emily felt at seeing her father's letters
is revived: ghosts of past family transgressions become the
major source of awful emotion. These letters, too, are ultimately
furnished with a rational and innocent explanation. It is only
Emily's over-sensitive imagination that has turned them into awful
crimes, her sensibility and predisposition to superstition making a
few lines from the letters into terrible secrets.

If *Udolpho* restores domesticity, virtue and reason to their proper places in the eighteenth-century order of things, it does so only at a price. By presenting vice, corruption and irrationality as evil in the text and as an effect of representations that produce over-sensitive imaginations, it also suggests that the values it espouses and reinforces are effects of representation as well. Like the unnatural or overly imaginative evils the novel tries to cast beyond the pale of good society, the moral and domestic values that it would like to naturalise are glimpsed as part of the fiction. *Udolpho's* attempt to externalise and expel all forms of vice and evil, including the excessive fancy and superstition encouraged by romances, leaves it, as a work of fiction itself, in an ambivalent position. Like the ambivalence perceived by critics in its overuse of suspense, there is a degree of uncertainty and instability in the way that the novel returns to conventional eighteenth-century values. This is of particular importance in respect of the roles given to women in the fiction. In many ways the text follows the moralistic pattern of eighteenth-century works like Richardson's *Clarissa* (1748–9) in its depictions of suffering virtue, to affirm values of domesticity and female propriety. In Radcliffe's novels, however, women are never completely confined to the home and family though, on one level, that is considered to be their proper place. Leaving the security of privileged domestic space, the female protagonists, and readers too, are supposed to learn, especially in the encounter with the violence and corruption of the outside world, of the advantages of family life. The escape from confine-ment, in narrative or reading, is no more than a prelude to a welcome return. The ambivalence remains, not only in the way that the home seems to conceal horrifying secrets but in the possibility that the escape, especially for readers, into imagined worlds and events may be more pleasurable than the return to domesticity. Indeed, throughout Radcliffe's novels, it is the heroines who, though subjugated, persecuted and imprisoned, still escape. Not only that, they and their reactions are the principal focus of the narrative. Apart from the malevolent villains, men play a very small and generally ineffectual part in the narratives. It is for these reasons that, despite the rational explanations and strongly moral conclusions, the distinctions of virtue and vice, good and evil, become rather precarious. While the former are advocated and brought within the sphere of domesticity and good society, the latter are never fully excluded or completely externalised.

TERROR NARRATIVES

Attempts to define and expunge vice in cautionary tales advocating virtue and family values were regularly repeated in the many novels which followed the model of Radcliffe's sentimentally-inflected Gothic romances. In stories of orphaned heroines with all the virtues of middle-class domestic values discovering their aristocratic birthright after a series of terrors, persecutions and imprisonments, readers were offered familiar plots, settings and protagonists. Though these became formulaic to the point of ridicule, there was often, as in Radcliffe, some degree of self-consciousness regarding the effects of romance and supernatural narratives. Regina Maria Roche was one of the most successful imitators of Radcliffe. Her novel *The Children of the Abbey* (1794) was almost as popular as *The Mysteries of Udolpho*. Another of Roche's novels, *Clermont* (1798), used a familiarly Radcliffean pattern, but found itself entangled in the ambivalence associated with Gothic narratives. *Clermont* is replete with decaying Gothic castles, ruined chapels, underground passages, dark forests and ghostly groanings. Its young heroine enjoys the tranquillity of rural life before suffering the terrors of cruelly unprincipled aristocrats and her own imagination. Mysterious events, ineffectual heroes and awful family secrets compose a novel that is made up of partial stories, letters and endless speculation. At the end, when the various stories are pieced together, vice is revealed for what it is and virtuous aristocratic identities are finally seen in their true and innocent light. Propriety and familial harmony is restored with a distinctly authorial declaration:

> 'The web of deceit is at length unravelled,' said St Julian, as soon as he concluded it, 'and the ways of Providence are justified to man. We now perceive, that however successful the schemes of wickedness may be at first, they are, in the end completely defeated and overthrown.'
>
> (p. 366)

The speaker is the heroine's father using his family name and occupying an aristocratic position to which he has only just been returned. For most of the novel he lives in guilty self-imposed exile. While a proper and patriarchal family order is restored and underwritten by Providence, its restoration is seen to be an effect of unravelling the stories, the 'webs of deceit', that make up most of the narrative. Demonstrating the dangers of being duped by the deceits of narrative, *Clermont* restores propriety only with difficulty.

Though the innocence of the father is finally explained it is his guilt that constitutes the awful secret of the tale. He is believed to have killed his half-brother. This crime is precipitated by his discovery, having grown up an orphan, of his true identity, an identity that he conceals from his daughter for most of the story, and the fact of his disinheritance. These crimes, alleged or otherwise, result from a tension that the novel tries to resolve. The tension between one's duty to one's family and one's own sentimental attachments is exacerbated by questions about the legitimacy of paternal authority. These questions horrify the heroine, Madeleine, as she begins to uncover her father's guilt. In endeavouring to disentangle the stories of the past the effects of narratives, horrid and otherwise, are brought to the fore. Stories and apparently supernatural events, like ghostly groanings and the mysterious appearance of a dagger, seem to point to the criminal past of Madeleine's father. When she confronts him he employs a conventional eighteenth-century set of terms to deflect the question: 'I trust my love,' cried he, 'you will not again listen to the idle surmises of the servants: even on the slightest foundation they are apt to raise improbabilities and horrors, which, in spite of reason, make too often a dangerous impression on the mind, and overturn its quiet, by engendering superstition' (p. 254). The Gothic father appeals to distinctly eighteenth-century criteria of judgement which depend on class distinctions. Servants, uneducated and uncultivated, are superstitious, they are the class that believe in horrors, not respectable women. This highlights a class division in readers assumed from Walpole onwards and implied in Radcliffe's manner of enlisting and simultaneously distancing readers from excesses of the imagination. In the 1790s, however, the shifting composition and appetites of the reading public made it a more difficult distinction to draw. It is, moreover, a distinction that is rendered suspect in *Clermont*. For the rumours that Madeleine's father disavows as superstition are, it later emerges, stories that he believes to be true. Clermont's implied denial is rendered more suspicious when he tells a different story to his own father. Confronted again by his daughter, he offers, not another story, but an appeal to values and character: 'I know your present ideas. But Oh, Madeleine! reflect on the tenor of my conduct, on the precepts I instilled into your mind and then think whether you have done me justice or injustice in harbouring them?' (p. 263). Unconvinced, Madeleine's suspicions might well be a result of the rational precepts she has learned from her father. Character, it seems, is an effect of narrative, not the reverse. Earlier, Madeleine's character has been judged on the basis of her narrative: 'your narrative, my dear, . . . convinces me more than ever of the innocence and sensibility of your disposition' (p. 56). Narratives, moreover, are the vehicles that propel Clermont towards his crime. Letters from his mother, and then a 'horrible narrative' deliberately intended to deceive him, rouse his passions into violent action. Suspicions about character and identity permeate the novel's reversals of apparently good and apparently bad characters. Even at the end the establishment of proper family places and identities depends on the stories and confessions of criminals. The figure, indeed, in whose name the web of deceit is unravelled and Providence invoked, has a different name and identity at the beginning.

Clermont finds it increasingly difficult to distinguish good and propriety from vice and evil because it acknowledges the importance of narratives in establishing, maintaining and legitimising the difference. The grounds for excluding, punishing and externalising vice become far less secure when they are implicated in narrative orders. Even as appeals are made to patriarchy and providential authority outside representation, there is a sense in which they are no longer credible in an enlightened and increasingly secular culture. Restoring, or, even, policing cultural distinctions requires an effort, a force that, in the works of Radcliffe and her imitators, is offered by the sublime. In Radcliffe's posthumously published essay 'On the Supernatural in Poetry' (1826), a development of Burke's aesthetic theory, the opposition that is established between terror and horror provides a useful delineation of different Gothic strategies: 'Terror and horror are so far opposite, that the first expands the soul, and awakens the faculties to a high degree of life; the other contracts, freezes, and nearly annihilates them' (p. 149). Radcliffe, as in her fiction, privileges terror over horror.

The elevation of terror, moreover, is made possible by a discrimination between the effects of obscurity and confusion, terms which, it is argued, are often used wrongly as synonyms by commentators. The difference is important: 'obscurity leaves something for the imagination to exaggerate; confusion, by blurring one image into another, leaves only a chaos in which the mind can find nothing to nourish its fears and doubts, or to act upon in any way' (p. 150). What is important is that terror activates the mind and the imagination, allowing it to overcome, transcend even, its fears and doubts, enabling the subject to move from a state of passivity to activity. This has important consequences: 'if obscurity has so much effect on fiction, what must it have in real life, when to ascertain the object of terror, is frequently to acquire the means of escaping it' (p. 150). Terror enables escape; it allows one to delimit its effects, to distinguish and overcome the threat it manifests. As in much fiction of the 1790s, it is by means of terror that the object of threat is escaped. Indeed, the threatening object can be cast out or away from the domain of rationality and domesticity and, as a result of this expulsion or externalisation, proper order can be reaffirmed as an order that exists outside narratives. By elevating the mind, objects of terror not only give it a sense of its own power but, in the appreciation of awful sublimity, suggest the power of a divine order, an order that, as Providence, is repeatedly invoked at the end of most Radcliffean novels as the way out of vice and the guarantee of conventional boundaries. In many works of Radcliffean Gothic terror enables a return to patterns of sentimental fiction.

HORROR

Horror, however, continually exerts its effects in tales of terror. Horror is most often experienced in underground vaults or burial chambers. It freezes human faculties, rendering the mind passive and immobilising the body. The cause is generally a direct encounter with physical mortality, the touching of a cold corpse, the sight of a decaying body. Death is presented as the absolute limit, a finitude which denies any possibility of imaginative tran-scendence into an awesome and infinite space. It is the moment of the negative sublime, a moment of freezing, contraction and horror which signals a temporality that cannot be recuperated by the mortal subject. Horror marks the response to an excess that cannot be transcended. It is why, despite the repeated attempts to contain Gothic machinery and effects within a dialectic of terror, the ambivalences of Radcliffean Gothic fiction can neither close satisfactorily nor fully externalise evil.

Horror never leaves the scene. In 1796, it emerged with greatest force in Matthew Lewis's *The Monk* and in the manner it was received. The scandal that greeted the novel's publication placed it among the most notorious works of English fiction. Considered dangerous in its obscenity, the text itself embodied a kind of horror. Its excesses, in part taken from Radcliffe, led to her own subsequent abandonment of much Gothic machinery: *The Italian*, published the year after *The Monk*, in 1797, can be seen as, if not exactly a reply to it, a cautious response to the scandal it created. The central figure of *The Italian* is a monk whose villainy and past crimes are never diabolical in a supernatural sense. Indeed, the whole novel moves away from the imagined terrors of Radcliffe's earlier works and towards a more credible and realistic narrative in direct contrast to *The Monk*. The latter goes in the other direction and, turning terror into horror, describes in lurid detail the spectres that Gothic fiction had previously left to the superstitious imagination or explained away.

The Monk eschews and satirises the sentimentality of Radcliffe's work. It draws instead on the *Sturm und Drang* (storm and stress) of German Romantic writers like Goethe and Schiller. During a visit to Germany Lewis met Goethe, and later showed his interest in German tales by translating several into English. He did the same with drama, capitalising on the vogue for the sensational in the theatre of the time. In the 1790s German writing was associated with the excessive emotionalism of Goethe's *Werther* or the shocks and horrors of robber tales by Schiller rather than virtuous sentimentality. The translator's preface to Flammenberg's *The Necromancer* (1794) recommended the text as one with 'wonderful incidents' and 'mysterious events' but without 'tiresome love intrigues'. Like Carl Grosse's German horror novel describing the mysterious workings of a powerful and sensually-inclined secret society, translated as *Horrid Mysteries* (1797), *The Necromancer* was included in the list of 'Horrid Novels' in *Northanger Abbey*.

While Lewis was influenced by the German tradition, *The Monk* is none the less traversed by contradictory, ambivalent impulses. The translator of *The Necromancer* recommends another, similar novel, that tells of 'a long series of frauds, perpetrated under the mysterious veil of pretended supernatural aid'. In stories like *The Necromancer*, the supernatural is revealed to be no more than hypocrisy or the concealment of very human crimes. In Lewis's novel one of the main targets is a hypocritical monk who conceals his vices beneath a cloak of sanctity. *The Monk*, however, does not refrain from vividly invoking supernatural elements. It often does so in a satirical or brutally mocking manner. The most celebrated incident of this kind occurs in one of the two parallel plots of the novel. Two lovers, Raymond and Agnes, decide to elope against the wishes of their families. To ensure the unimpeded escape of Agnes, they decide to dress her in the habit of a spectral nun believed to haunt the castle. In the course of the elopement their coach crashes and Agnes disappears. The injured Raymond is put to bed and sees, not Agnes, but the actual ghost of the nun. He is petrified with horror. Lewis's marvellous twist to the conventions of the Gothic tale is indicative of *The Monk*'s ambivalence as it interweaves horror with a general mockery of the genre. The other ambiguous use of the supernatural in the novel occurs at its end with the appearance of the devil to claim the soul of Ambrosio. As a figure of supernatural justice punishing the sinful monk with eternal damnation, the devil's appearance marks out the Faustian form of the novel with a cautionary note about the dangers of giving in to the forces of desire. Critics, however, were far from convinced by the moral tone of the ending. Indeed, the over-exaggerated style of the punishment works against its supposed avowal of morality and suggests that the cautionary note is merely a weak, even satirical, get-out clause for a novel overindulged in immorality and excess.

The Monk is about excess, about excesses of passion concealed beneath veils of respectability and propriety. It uses the conventional anti-Catholicism of Gothic fiction implied in the monastic setting, but it is the tyrannical nature of, and barbaric superstitions inculcated by, all institutions, including aristocracy, Church and family, that forms the general object of criticism. Institutional repression is seen to encourage excess. Family prohibitions produce illicit passions and lead to the imprisonment of recalcitrant members, particularly women, in convents. The spectral nun is the ghost of a female transgressor from the family past of Raymond and Agnes. Justice is harsh and often violently retributive. Religious superstition is similarly rigorous in its policing of social behaviour.

The principal figure of excess is Ambrosio, the monk of the novel's title. He is famed as the most pious and saintly of monks, and crowds flock, adoringly, to attend his sermons. His pride in his own sanctity blinds him to his ambitions and passions. The account of Ambrosio's fall into passion provides both the sensational and sensual aspects of the novel. These take place in the gloomy labyrinthine vaults beneath the Abbey. Ambrosio's lust initially finds an object in Mathilda, a young woman, infatuated with him, who disguises herself as a novice monk called Rosario in order to enter the same institution. Strangely attracted to Rosario, Ambrosio finally gives in to the very literal temptations of the flesh when Mathilda unveils herself before him. Then Ambrosio directs his desires towards another woman, Antonia. Pure, innocent and belonging to a noble family, she seems an impossible object. Mathilda offers her help, declaring herself to be an agent of the devil. She leads a hesitant Ambrosio through the underground vaults so that he can make the diabolical pact that will ensure the satisfaction of his lusts. The gratification of his carnal appetites involves killing Antonia's mother and spiriting the innocent victim to a secret chamber deep in the underground vaults. There Ambrosio seduces her and then learns that she is his sister. The passion and violence does not finish with this horror. Rumours of Ambrosio's, and other, crimes committed in the monastery provoke outrage among the populace and an angry mob sets about its destruction.

The Monk, similar in terms of its lavish sensual descriptions, its violent images and extravagant scenes to *Vathek*, met with a very different reception. It gave rise to a new and diabolical strand of Gothic fiction, evident in the numbers of 'monk' novels that followed it. T. J. Horsley-Curties drew on Radcliffe and Lewis in the title of his romance *The Monk of Udolpho* (1807). Charlotte Dacre, in *Zofloya; or, the Moor* (1806), used the theme of Faustian damnation in a story of a female villain tempted by a black agent of the devil. While *Vathek* was considered a moral tale, *The Monk* was perceived as an outright obscenity. The reviewer for the *Monthly Review* (1797) argued that 'a vein of obscenity' pervaded and deformed the whole novel, making it 'unfit for general circulation' (p. 451). Coleridge, in the *Critical Review* (1796), stated 'that the Monk is a romance, which if a parent saw in the hands of a son or a daughter, he might reasonably turn pale'. He went on to describe the 'libidinous minuteness' and the 'voluptuous images' of the novel as 'poison for youth, and a provocative for the debauchee' (p. 197). As an affront to moral, family and Christian values, the novel's potential for corrupting young minds was a particular fear. What exacerbated the potential of its obscene and lewd descriptions was, as a number of critics noted, the elegance of the style. This seems to have contributed to concerns about its poisonous effects on young and undiscriminating minds. Expressing several reservations, the *Analytical Review* (1796) observed that the novel elicited the reader's sympathy for Ambrosio (p. 403). The possibility of identifying with such a figure no doubt contributed to the very ambiguous morality of the novel. Its lack of a clearly stated and convincing moral, moreover, demanded that it be severely criticised. The exclusion of the novel parallels the exclusions of evil figures in previous works of Gothic fiction. Ambrosio and *The Monk*, however, testify to the continuing difficulty of the process of externalising evil.

There were other reasons that accounted for the savage critical reception. One was that Lewis included, along with his name on the title page, the initials 'MP': he had just been elected to Parliament. Coleridge responded to this detail: 'the author of the Monk signs himself a LEGISLATOR! We stare and tremble' (p. 198). It was not only the position and literary skills of the author that made the novel such an object of anxiety. In the middle of the 1790s there were more serious threats to social and domestic stability with which certain parts of *The Monk* must have had a degree of resonance: its description of the riotous mob destroying the monastery, for example, is likely to have been read alongside accounts of revolutionary mobs in France.

LABYRINTHS OF LITERATURE AND POLITICS

It is in T. J. Matthias's *The Pursuits of Literature* (1796) that novels and romances are closely linked to the threat of revolution spreading across the channel from France. In encouraging appetites for excitement and sensation and thereby disturbing the balance of domestic harmony and moral propriety, the effects of novels and romances were associated with the passions and violence of Revolutionary mobs in France. One polemical statement among the many that punctuate *The Pursuits of Literature* makes the nature of the connection explicit: 'Our *unsexed* female writers now instruct, or confuse, us and themselves in the labyrinths of politics, or turn us wild with Gallic frenzy' (p. 244). Departing from the strictures of reason and morality, novels are seen to cause violent frenzy as terrifying as that exhibited in France. By touching on political subjects women writers 'unsex' themselves: they enter with impunity and impropriety a male domain of writing instead of remaining within the domesticated limits of fiction. The metaphor of the labyrinth is also crucial in its articulation of literature, politics and Gothic romances. Earlier in the eighteenth century, in writings by Smollett, Pope and Fielding, the labyrinth or maze was used as a figure signifying the complexity and variety of society which remained, none the less, unified. It was a positive term. In Gothic romances, however, it came to be associated with fear, confusion and alienation: it was a site of darkness, horror and desire. In the labyrinthine vaults of *The Monk* Ambrosio begins his descent into infamy and a pact with the devil. At one point, torn between fear and desire, he almost gives in to conscience and his own horror at what he is about to do. Reflecting on the impossibility of escaping his physical imprisonment in the dark and winding passages, he also understands that he cannot escape or master the desires that have brought him so far. His doubts, fears, dilemmas and helplessness in this labyrinth render him passive like a Gothic heroine. Giving in to lust, however, he begins his transformation into a Gothic villain. This role is exemplified when, again in the secret depths of the labyrinth, Ambrosio prepares to consummate his desire and violate Antonia. In the labyrinth, hidden and separated from the laws of the outside world, he is, as he makes clear to Antonia, absolute master. Imprisoned in the labyrinth, she is cut off from all aid and society, dead to the world.

The horror of the labyrinth and its confusion of fears and desires lies in its utter separation from all social rules and complete transgression of all conventional limits. In *The Italian* Vivaldi, the hero, is imprisoned by the Inquisition and led to trial in the heart of an underground labyrinth. He describes its horror: 'along the galleries, and other avenues through which they passed, not any person was seen, and, by the profound stillness that reigned, it seemed as if death had already anticipated his work in these regions of horror, and condemned alike the tortured and the torturer' (p. 309). Death, as absolute disconnection from any form of order, signifies the complete alienation of individuals in a finite world. In *Clermont*, moreover, it is narratives that are labyrinthine, spinning their 'web of deceit' and leading protagonists to encounter the horrible absence, the death, of any familiar or proper order.

The labyrinth presented in *The Pursuits of Literature* is, ironically, a distinctly Gothic locus and works in a manner akin to Radcliffe's doubled narratives. Its horrors, moreover, are intensified by their association with political terrors. Matthias's text praises the well-known conservative positions of Burke and the Abbe Barruel who unmasked the conspirators – the secret societies and radical philosophers – who were believed to have plotted the whole Revolution. It takes a polemical stance towards revolution, reform and democracy: all forms of change lead to revolution, embodied in France as site of sedition, anarchy, heresy, deception, confusion, superstitious corruption, wickedness, lust, cruelty and destruction. France is '*THE MONSTROUS REPUBLIC*' (p. 164). Modern philosophers, like Rousseau, Paine and Godwin, are identified as subversive, as are all radicals and freethinkers. Novels by Charlotte Smith and Fanny Burney are criticised for overstepping the 'boundaries of nature and real life' (p. 58), a transgression which has political implications when linked to accusations that texts by Elizabeth Inchbald and Mary Robinson turn girls' heads 'wild with impossible adventures' and leave them 'now and then tainted with democracy' (p. 56). Gothic novels, with the exception of Radcliffe's works, receive short shrift. *The Monk*, however, receives attention as a publication 'too important to be passed over in a general reprehension' (p. 245). Particular offence is taken against the novel's unashamed depiction of 'the arts of lewd and systematic seduction' and its 'unqualified blasphemy'; concern is expressed that it has not been prosecuted for obscenity. Horrified that Lewis is a Member of Parliament, Matthias finds no excuse in his youth and no relief in the defence that the novel contains many 'poetical descriptions': 'so much the worse again, the novel is more alluring on that account. Is it a time to poison the waters of our land in their springs and fountains? Are we to add incitement to incitement, and corruption to corruption, till there neither is, nor can be, a return to virtuous action and regulated life?' (pp. 248–9). Style as much as content is, as with many criticisms of the Gothic novel, the main source of anxiety. Style seduces readers, leads them astray and leaves them unable to distinguish between virtue and vice and thereby expel the latter. Lewis's style inspired sympathy for Ambrosio, also rendering moral judgement equivocal and the externalisation of evil difficult to sustain.

The ambivalence that emerges in respect of questions of style and content has consequences for conceptions of the place and function of literature. Matthias's attacks on unacceptable literary production, and their intensity, are explained by the importance and the ambivalence of literary texts in the preservation or disruption of social values and political order: 'LITERATURE, *well or ill-conducted*, is THE GREAT ENGINE, *by which all* civilized *states must ultimately be supported or overthrown*' (p. 162). Repeated later in *The Pursuits of Literature*, the statement makes plain a bifurcation that Matthias wishes to make absolute in order to sustain literature's properly ideological role. His attempt to distinguish supportive from subversive literature, however, leads him into those strangely Gothic labyrinths wherein a Radcliffean strategy is used to find an exit. Labyrinths, as places of radical politics and confusion, are identified as dangerous, subversive sites destroying established boundaries and conventions. Linked to novels that raise the contaminating spectre of democracy and excite readers with a 'Gallic frenzy' that simultaneously upsets proper national and sexual identifications, the labyrinth is also associated with confusion, deception and 'superstitious corruption'. These Protestant constructions of a tyrannical and superstitious Catholicism are combined in the attack on radicals and revolutionary conspirators, adding force and negative signifi-cance to the labyrinth in the process. A place of all forms of excessive, irrational and passionate behaviour, the labyrinth is also the site in which the absence or loss of reason, sobriety, decency and morality is displayed in full horror. *The Pursuits of Literature* sets out to guide its readers through the labyrinth in order to secure 'to this kingdom her political and religious existence, and the rights of society'. It is thus on a mission of life and death that Matthias tenders his services as guide:

> It is designed to conduct them through the labyrinths of literature; to convince them of the manner in which the understanding and affections are either bewildered, darkened, ennervated, or degraded; and to point out the fatal paths which would lead us all to final destruction, or to complicated misery.
>
> (p. 3)

Labyrinths, like novels, seduce, excite, confuse and disturb; they lead readers on 'fatal paths'. Matthias's account describes both narrative form and narrative effects. These have to be endured in order to be escaped, offering a knowledge that will allow their potential destruction to be avoided. Guided through the dark labyrinth, like a Radcliffean heroine, and confronting its dangers – losses of understanding, proper affection, equanimity, virtue and life itself – produces, by means of a horrified recoil, a recognition of Matthias's call to preserve the existence of the religious, domestic and political order of the country.

The journey through the labyrinth that is undertaken becomes as difficult and divisive as any in Gothic fiction. Matthias's position as both guide and reader duplicates the ambivalent tendencies of the Radcliffean narrative. To provoke a sense of horror Matthias invites superstitious and overactive imaginings on the part of the reader 'in which the understanding and affections are either bewildered, darkened, ennervated, or degraded'. This leads to the emotional recoil that dispels the magical illusions with rational explanation. A *frisson* of terror leads to the return of reason. This operation, however, inextricably binds literature's supportive function to its subversive potential. This is evident in Matthias's account of reading the work of radical philosophers:

> Philosophy has appeared, not to console but to deject. When I have read and thought deeply on the accumulated horrors,

and on all the gradations of wickedness and misery, through
which the modern systematic philosophy of Europe has
conducted her illuminated votaries to the confines of political
death and mental darkness, my mind for a space feels a
convulsion, and suffers the nature of an insurrection.

(pp. 17–18)

Rational assurance confronts horror as Matthias is drawn into the
corrupting labyrinth of philosophy. This benighted, fatal world is
exactly like that described in Gothic fiction, only with radicals
having taken the place of monks and villains. Similarly, Matthias's
response mimics that of a Gothic heroine encountering the horrors
of the labyrinth, either in the form of a decaying corpse or as her
own alienation from the world of conventions and normality.

Acknowledging the power of texts to produce convulsion or
insurrection in the rational mind, Matthias depends on an excess
of feeling to restore reason to its privileged place. The horror
depicted in his account, like Radcliffe's, is designed to produce
similar effects. As a warning about the dangers of texts, *The
Pursuits of Literature* presents a world of death as the consequence
of any social, political or literary deviation. The duplication
of Gothic patterns remains ambivalent. In the labyrinth Matthias
reaches the bewildered and enervated limits of his own understanding, losing his reason in a convulsion of horror, a sublime
encounter with his own limits and those of social value.
Duplicating the divided position offered by Gothic texts, as both
rational and imaginative, knowing and superstitiously emotional,
the convulsion of horror borders on the 'Gallic frenzy' he fears will
be produced by the texts of 'unsexed female writers'. Distinctions
that hold rational, sexual and moral identities in place are
threatened by the labyrinth's confusions. Representation and its
ambivalent powers to stabilise, seduce and subvert come to the
fore. The force of representation in maintaining order, moreover,
involves a reinscription of Gothic patterns and strategies. In

Matthias's text France and the French are constructed along the lines of Gothic narratives. Not only subjects of Catholicism's 'superstitious corruption', Frenchmen are thoroughly Gothic in their villainy: 'always brutal', '*neighing* after the constitution of their neighbours, in their lawless lustihood', 'they first deflower the purity of the struggling or half-consenting victims, and then with their ruffian daggers they stifle at once the voice, and the remembrance of the pollution. Such are their abominations; such are their orgies of blood and lust' (p. 4). Magnifications of Gothic bandits and villains in every respect, French men are represented as the outcome of any deviance from order.

The Gothic figures that are invoked not only testify to the power of narratives and representation in sustaining political and social order, but display the conservative function of sublimity and history in the process. The tone and intensity of Matthias's text is drawn from its main influence, Burke's *Reflections on the Revolution in France* (1790). Burke's reaction to the threat he sees emanating from France and from radicals in England itself invokes a Gothic form of narrative. Given the influence of Burke's theories of the sublime and the beautiful on many Gothic writers, especially Radcliffe, it is hardly surprising that his writings on the French Revolution are painted in powerfully monochromatic hues. His reflections on the revolution construct events in France as a darkly sublime threat in contrast to the gently enlightened tones of English social and political stability. In the darkest colours of confusion, obscurity and selfish passion, the new social formation ushered in by the Revolution is seen as a chaotic assemblage of vice, depravity, self-interest and commercial opportunism: France's 'monster of a constitution' gives free reign to 'attornies, agents, money-jobbers, speculators, and adventurers, composing an ignoble oligarchy founded upon the destruction of the crown, the church, the nobility, and the people. Here end all the deceitful dreams and visions of the equality and rights of men' (p. 313). All ideas and writings advocating revolution or reform, in England as well as

France, are associated with the 'monstrous fiction' that Burke sees enacted in France. Wanting to countermand the 'deceitful dreams and visions' of radicals, Burke's text acknowledges the forces of social and political change and anxiously produces his own representation, his own fiction, in opposition.

Burke's defence of constitutional monarchy, aristocracy, landed property and the Church as the bases for an ordered society takes the form of a nostalgic romance imbued with chivalric values. Vividly presenting an account of the capture of the French Queen by a riotous mob, Burke bemoans the absence of gallantry that left her undefended and waxes lyrical about the time he viewed the splendours of the French court: 'I thought ten thousand swords must have leaped from their scabbards to avenge even a look that threatened her with insult. – But the age of chivalry is gone. – That of sophisters, oeconomists, and calculators, has succeeded; and the glory of Europe is extinguished for ever' (p. 170). The French Revolution turns into a Gothic romance. The role of the heroine clearly delineated, that of the villain falls to the French Assembly: 'they have power given to them, like that of an evil principle, to subvert and destroy; but none to construct, except such machines as maybe fitted for further subversion and further destruction' (p. 161). The romantic polarisation of good and evil enables the renunciation of all things French and therefore evil. The polarisation, however, involves the reinvigoration of romance fictions in order to combat those of English and French radicals: as with Gothic novels, it is representation that is both at stake and the crucial weapon in the contest. Burke's appeal to a romance tradition attempts to establish a sense of continuous history and awake a series of associations that wrest words like freedom, nation and order from the grasp of radical texts. It also imagines the dissolution of English society in order that readers' terror, like his own, at the events in France, will completely purge their minds of any radical ideas. The evil in France and in radical writings is expelled from the shores of England.

The language Burke uses, and the meanings of Gothic he draws upon, have particular political associations with a Whig tradition that emerged in the later seventeenth century. In this context Gothic signified the northern European tribes, admired for their love of freedom and democratic institutions. In using this Gothic significance to support English institutions of monarchy, family and government, Burke pre-empts radical calls for democracy and political equality by suggesting that the continuity of English tradition has already established them. A very different sense of the word Gothic is employed by many of the English writers who spring to the defence of radicalism in response to Burke's *Reflections*: for Thomas Paine and Mary Wollstonecraft, two radicals who responded to Burke's revolutionary polemics with accusations directed at his Gothic ideas, the term signified, quite conventionally, everything that was old-fashioned, barbaric, feudal and irrationally ungrounded. In *The Rights of Man* (1791–2), Paine uses Burke's lament at the passing of the age of chivalry to criticise the *Reflections* as a piece of imaginative and evocative fiction in the manner of a drama or quixotic romance. Paine's main political targets are the institutions and customs Burke defends: despotic government and its arbitrary power, religious authority, hypocrisy and property, aristocracy, its insistence on primogeniture and its hereditary privileges. Wollstonecraft, also, is critical of Burke's 'Gothic' ideas and the way they reinforce an uncivilised and dehumanising set of values and socio-economic practices. In her *A Vindication of the Rights of Men* (1790), Wollstonecraft criticises the lack of humanity and liberality implied in Burke's position: 'Man preys on man; and you mourn for the idle tapestry that decorated a gothic pile, and the dronish bell that summoned the fat priest to prayer' (p. 58). Linked to the religious superstitions and hypocrisies of Catholicism that were a permanent feature of Gothic works, Burke's lack of rationality and humanity is seen as a defence of a barbaric aristocracy, savage property laws and feudal injustice. For radicals, all that is Gothic is signified by the *ancien régime* in France. Defending the French National Assembly against Burke's attacks Wollstonecraft again uses Gothic associations as a form of insult: 'Why was it a duty to repair an ancient castle, built in barbarous ages, of Gothic materials? Why were the legislators obliged to rake among heterogeneous ruins . . . ?' (p. 41). In Wollstonecraft's rational humanism, the mention of Burke's Gothic nostalgia can only be an insult. These invocations of the word Gothic in defences of revolution were written before the Terror in France gave new weight to those conservative writers of tales of terror in England.

The continuing ambivalence and polarisation of the word Gothic until the end of the eighteenth century was significant not only in the changes of meaning that it underwent but in its function in a network of associations whose positive or negative value depended on the political positions and representations with which Gothic figures were associated. Indeed, the Gothic figures that appeared in so many novels, as well as critical, aesthetic and political discussions, became signs of a pervasive cultural anxiety concerning the relation of present and past, and the relationship between classes, sexes and individuals within society. Gothic figures were also indicative of changing notions of culture and nature. Markers of a lost order or of a feudal practice that continued to oppress people, the castles, counts and monks of Gothic fiction remained politically ambivalent, seen as figures of nostalgia or criticism. The term itself was a site of struggle and an effect of contests to represent an authoritative, singular and legitimate version of identity, sexuality, culture and its history. As such, invocations of the word Gothic could not fail to be ambivalent, could not fail to disclose as much as they tried to discard, bringing questions of evil and vice to the fore as political constructs, themselves dependent on partial and politically interested representations. The problem of locating, defining and policing the effects of representations bound Gothic writing and history to a political arena in which singularity and order vanished into mythical pasts. Threats to society and convention that were depicted in Gothic terms altered notions of representation and literature beyond repair. From being a way of containing and warning against vices, evils and antisocial behaviour, Gothic romances became advocates of subversion. Irreparably divided, tortuously ambivalent, these narratives could only attempt to maintain conventions and identities by repeating, identifying and externalising examples of evil in a movement that embraced their own narrative form. Under pressure from contradictory demands, those narrative forms, moreover, began to change in the 1790s. From identifying villains and practices to be excluded as vicious or evil, narratives ceded to the ambivalence that shaped them and became increasingly uncertain of the location of evil and vice. In the 1790s, as fears of Gothic fiction are bound up more and more with processes of representation, the locus of evil vacillates between outcast individuals and the social conventions that produced or constricted them.

5

ROMANTIC TRANSFORMATIONS

She was an elfin Pinnace; lustily
I dipped my oars into the silent lake;
And, as I rose upon the stroke, my boat
Went heaving through the Water like a swan:
When, from behind that craggy Steep, till then
The horizon's bound, a huge peak, black and huge,
As if with voluntary power instinct,
Upreared its head. – I struck, and struck again,
And, growing still in stature, the grim Shape
Towered up between me and the stars, and still,
For so it seemed, with purpose of its own
And measured motion, like a living Thing
Strode after me.
(William Wordsworth, *The Prelude* (1850), Bk I, ll. 373–85)

In the period dominated by Romanticism, Gothic writing began to move inside, disturbing conventional social limits and notions of interiority and individuality. The internalisation of Gothic forms represents the most significant shift in the genre, the gloom and darkness of sublime landscapes becoming external markers of inner mental and emotional states. Many Gothic elements found their way into the work of writers from Wordsworth to Keats, though the significance and resonance of Gothic devices and themes were undergoing notable transformations. While the standard plots and narrative machinery – as established by Walpole, Radcliffe and Lewis – continued to be imitated in many novels and stories well into the nineteenth century, major innovations, or renovations, of the genre drew it closer to aspects of Romanticism.

It is at the level of the individual that Romantic-Gothic writing takes its bearings. The individual in question stands at the edges of society and rarely finds a path back into the social fold. The critical distance taken with regard to social values derives from radical attacks on oppressive systems of monarchical government. Instead, the consciousness, freedom and imagination of the subject is valued. Usually male, the individual is outcast, part victim, part villain. Older Gothic figures and devices, overused to the point of cliché, are transformed into signs of aristocratic tyranny, leftovers from an unenlightened world. The disturbing and demonic villain, however, retains a darkly attractive, if ambivalent, allure as a defiant rebel against the constraints of social mores. The sympathies for suffering, doomed individuals find expression in Romantic identifications with Prometheus and Milton's Satan, regarded as heroes because of their resistance to overpowering tyranny. The villain or outcast, unlike much Radcliffean writing, is not the cause of evil and terror, an object to be execrated so that order can be restored. It is a position which calls for respect and understanding. Real evil is identified among embodiments of tyranny, corruption and prejudice, identified with certain, often aristocratic, figures and, more frequently, with institutions of power manifested in government hierarchies, social norms and religious superstition.

The prevailing narrative forms accord with the focus on Romantic individuals. First-person tales highlight the psychological interest in the dilemmas and suffering that attend social alienation. Subject as they are to imaginations, passions and fears they can neither control nor overcome, the heroes' imaginative trans-gressions of conventional values encounter the limits, laws, rules and forces that are not their own. Seekers after knowledge of themselves and metaphysical powers beyond and in deified nature, these individuals can be associated with the way that notions of human identity, mental and natural powers were being trans-formed and secularised, not only in political theory but also in the scientific disoveries of the time. In political terms, the failure of the French Revolution to realise hopes for human progress and equality contributed to the inward and darkening turn of Romantic speculations. Alienated from society and themselves, Romantic-Gothic heroes undergo the effects of this disillusion, doubting the nature of the powers that consume them, uncertain whether they originate internally or from external forces. Without an adequate social framework to sustain a sense of identity, the wanderer encounters the new form of the Gothic ghost, the double or shadow of himself. An uncanny figure of horror, the double presents a limit that cannot be overcome, the representation of an internal and irreparable division in the individual psyche.

PERSECUTORY ROMANCE

In his *Enquiry Concerning Political Justice* (1793), William Godwin describes the feudal system as a 'voracious monster', the remnant of which in the eighteenth century continues to bolster aristocratic power and privilege in the form of a stuffed monster that terrifies humankind into 'patience and pusillanimity' (p. 476). A small but important part of the book's radical and rationalist attack on forms of government riddled with relics of a feudal past in the shape of monarchy, courts and inherited wealth, the metaphor of the monster highlights the barbarity and tyranny of feudal power. The figure of the stuffed monster, moreover, stresses both the extinction of feudal economic power and its strange persistence at a superstructural level. As a stuffed monster, aristocratic power is an illusion, a phantom of a barbaric and superstitious past that lingers, forcefully, in the present. The terrors seem at once real and imaginary, strangely effective yet ungrounded and insubstantial. In the reaction to the Revolution in France, the monster had very real effects: laws were passed enabling the suppression of radical texts and the arrest, imprisonment and persecution of radicals.

In *Caleb Williams* (1794), written immediately after *Political Justice* and originally entitled *Things as They Are*, Godwin detailed the oppressions that existed in the society of the time. Injustice and persecution, very real issues in the novel, are also imaginary in the wider sense implied by the stuffed monster: they describe the terrifying and superstitious beliefs that irrationally persist and govern ideas about and actions in the world. In the trial scene of *Caleb Williams*, where Caleb is falsely accused of stealing from his master, he is called a monster when he rejects the findings of the mock court which condemns and frames him, his disrespect for the law and the title of 'gentleman' earning him the appellation and the identity of outcast. The greater monstrosity, the real horror, however, is that presented in the first-person narrative as the recognition of the injustices and crimes that can be committed in the name of the law. The metaphor of the stuffed monster links politics and fiction by associating feudalism and tales of terror with the persistence of superstitious, barbaric and irrational values. In this respect *Caleb Williams* criticises the Gothic romance as an oppressive and conservative form. The novel none the less uses Gothic strategies, not satirically, but politically to display social and psychological oppression.

The novel assembles various stories in its account of what *Political Justice* describes as 'the Gothic and unintelligible burden' borne by readers of romance and inheritors of feudalism (p. 477). While the first-person narrator, Caleb, an orphan taken in as secretary to squire Falkland, is the central figure later in the novel, his master provides the principal interest at the start. Caleb collects stories of Falkland's past which testify to his talents, generosity, grace and benevolence, qualities that make him popular in local society, much to the chagrin of another squire, Tyrell, who, brutish, tyrannical, selfish and uncultured, is Falkland's aristocratic antithesis. Their rivalry culminates in the murder of Tyrell. Tried for the crime, Falkland is acquitted, other victims of Tyrell's cruelty being blamed and hung.

Caleb, suspicious of his master's moody behaviour, eventually draws a confession from him. The truth has a price for Caleb has sold himself 'to gratify a foolishly inquisitive humour' (p.142). Charged to remain forever in the service of a master who hates him, Caleb is subjected to external forms of discipline and surveillance in the shape of Falkland and the legal and aristocratic code that protects him. This surveillance is also internalised. Tormented by the secret, 'a source of perpetual melancholy', Caleb says he has made himself a prisoner of guilt as well as the caprices of his master: 'the vigilance even of a public and systematical despotism is poor, compared with a vigilance which is thus goaded by the most anxious passions of the soul' (p. 144). Daring neither to flee Falkland's power nor able to stay under its subjugation, the novel describes Caleb's sufferings under both forms of vigilance as he tries to escape an unbearable double bind.

The dilemma and self-divisions are intensified by the manner in which external and internal persecutory vigilance is shown to be an effect of Caleb's identification with Falkland. His crime of spying against Falkland is a crime against his own self, modelled on an idealised version of his master: his guilt is defined in terms of the values he has internalised from this ideal. Attempting to escape the unbearable physical and psychical imprisonment, Caleb enlists the help of Falkland's brother-in-law, Forrester. Trusting in the latter, Caleb returns to be disbelieved, framed for theft and imprisoned. The prison conditions suffered by Caleb before his trial, echoing the darkness and coldness of Gothic dungeons, foreground the horrors of judicial systems. In distinct contrast is the band of thieves joined by Caleb after his escape. They are modelled on Schiller's Romantic robbers, 'thieves without a licence . . . at open war with another set of men who are thieves according to law' (p. 224). Rational, democratic and humanitarian principles among thieves reflect critically on wider society's pretensions to justice.

In one of the reversals that dominate the novel, a member of the band, Gines, becomes the agent of Falkland's persecution of Caleb, hounding him wherever he goes, no matter what identity he assumes. A decisive turn by Caleb, however, brings the novel to its climax: he decides to challenge Falkland in court and, tortured by guilt and self-loathing, to shatter the codes of secrecy and honour fatally binding his master and himself together. By now the dual relationship of master and servant has a bleaker aspect: Falkland is a broken man, a ghostly remnant of his former self worn down by guilt and publicly admitting his villainy. Ideals are sacrificed, reputations obviously false: in their self-loathing and betrayal, Caleb and his master are again doubles of each other, not ideal images, but inverted mirrors, shadows of suffering and persecution. Once the antithesis of Tyrell, the disclosure of Falkland's murderous secret makes him the same agent of irrationality and oppression. Caleb, the initiator and victim of the vigilance in his spying on Falkland, casts himself as both victim and villain who, in destroying his previously idealised master, destroys himself: 'I began these memoirs with the idea of vindicating my character. I have now no character that I wish to vindicate' (p. 337).

In the original ending of the novel Caleb is again imprisoned and injustice continues. The revised version sees Falkland die and Caleb become the living gravestone of a human being. In both versions, however, there appears no way out of the imprisonment embodied by the first-person narrative itself, for that would be to return to conventional and Gothic narrative frames that are challenged throughout the novel. Falkland is a figure from a Gothic romance, marked by his ideals of chivalry, honour and personal reputation. He speaks 'the language of romance' (p. 182), becomes a 'fool of fame' (p. 141) and, having imbibed the 'poison of chivalry', is driven to passion and violence like a Gothic villain: 'Begone, devil! . . . or I will trample you into atoms', he cries in a characteristically demonic manner (p. 10). The assumption of terrifying power is reiterated later in threats against Caleb (p. 150). In the novel, these internal states and individual statements indicating psychical delusions, paranoia and persecution are coloured in more distinct Gothic terms than external persecution. Imprisonment and injustice is a real horror that needs little Gothic colouring, whereas the turmoil induced by alienation and mental suffering appear in more menacing shades. *Caleb Williams*'s use of Gothic extremes also reflects, like much of the novel, on the poisonous, alienating and imprisoning effects of narrative: much of Caleb's persecution is enacted through the circulation of false stories, leading to his expulsion from secure communities and the necessity of assuming different false identities. His torment is in part to live a life without unified or authentic identity, supporting a 'counterfeit character' that reduces him to bestial degradation (p. 265). External forms, deceptive, inhuman and evil, lead to alienation, guilt and self-destruction, in which values of humanity, justice and identity are left in torturous doubt. With social forms as corrupt, unjust and persecutory as they are in *Caleb Williams*, the horror seems to be that there is no alternative or resolution to the unbearable conflicts that are produced.

Internal conflicts and external contradictions, the play of ideals, deception and duplicity recur in Godwin's other novels. Addressed in historical, romantic and fantastic modes, the outcasts and wanderers are, like Caleb, both agents and victims of their conditions, drawn by pride and passion, by social prejudice and accidents of circumstance to transgress convention. In Godwin's fifth novel, *St Leon* (1799), the promise of the elixir of life and the philosopher's stone turns out to be a curse that leaves the immortal wanderer isolated from all comforts of family and society. Bringing Faustian elements of Gothic fiction to the fore and alchemists from a feudal past into the present, the novel highlights the way human aspirations to knowledge, wealth, certainty and power become impossible, exclusive ideals that return to the despair and alienation depicted in *Caleb Williams*.

ROMANTIC HEROES

The hopeless and doomed quest of a cursed wanderer in *St Leon* discloses a darker current within the Romantic imagination's visions of unity and transcendence, a Gothic strain that inhabits much of the period's poetry. The darker, agonised aspect of Romantic writing has heroes in the Gothic mould: gloomy, isolated and sovereign, they are wanderers, outcasts and rebels condemned to roam the borders of social worlds, bearers of a dark truth or horrible knowledge, like Coleridge's Ancient Mariner. Milton's Satan or Prometheus are transgressors who represent the extremes of individual passion and consciousness. Blake's mythical creations, the tyrant Urizen and the suffering Los, inhabit a violent world of fire and struggle. Drawing on the anti-rational and mystical powers associated with a bardic romance tradition, Blake's poetic mythology values liberty, especially of the imagination, above any restraint, particularly of religious and political institutions. Byron's heroes, and his own impersonation of the Byronic hero, possess the defiant energy of a Gothic villain. In 'Manfred' (1817) the disenchanted solitary defies the powers of natural and spirit worlds. He is alienated from humankind:

> From my youth upwards
> My spirit walked not with the souls of men,
> Nor look'd upon the earth with human eyes;
>
> (II, 50–2)

Seeking something more than quotidian existence, he pursues the secrets of alchemical thought:

> And then I dived,
> In my lone wanderings, to the caves of death,
> Searching its cause in its effect; and drew
> From wither'd bones, and skulls, and heap'd up dust,
> Conclusions most forbidden.

(II, 79–83)

He quests in vain: existence remains unbearable to 'fools of time and terror' (II, 164) for the ideal form of his lost love is irrecuperable, even when conjured up by mysterious and magical powers. The setting of the verse drama, too, is important: the awe and terror inspired by the sublimity of wild, mountainous realms not only signifies a grandeur beyond human powers, but mirrors the internal world of the heroic sufferer, the magnificence of his suffering. In the throes of excessive feeling and tormented consciousness Romantic subjectivity is mystified as the shadowy image of the grander forces of natural creation and destruction or the mysterious power of the imagination.

Percy Shelley's 'Alastor' (1816), the story of a Romantic solitary in search of his ideal, uses wild, mountainous and stormy settings to present an external image of the alienated wanderer. His youthful literary efforts included two Gothic novels, *Zastrozzi* (1810) and *St Irvyne* (1811). He returned to Gothic themes in 'The Cenci' (1820). This poem, recounting the story of a debauched and vicious father whose cruelty and incestuous passions drive his victim, his daughter, to murder, has a recognisably Gothic framework in its themes of parental wickedness and filial suffering. Shelley, moreover, is quick to make the link between domestic and political tyranny. Following the Godwinian model, in which individual crime is set in the context of wider social forces, Shelley contrasts the daughter's suffering at the hands of the state with the protection the father received throughout his life while pursuing his nefarious activities. The daughter's punishment compounds the injustice embedded in domestic and political institutions.

In other poems of the Romantic period the use of romance forms, language and settings connects the writing more directly with the medieval poetic tradition used by Gothic writers to give Romantic themes of individualism and naturalism an atmosphere of strangeness and mystical distance. Byron's *Childe Harold's Pilgrimage* (1812–16) is subtitled 'A Romaunt', an archaic rendering of romance. The use of medieval language and Spenserian stanzas adds to the archaic atmosphere in the account of the wanderings of the 'shameless wight/ Sore given to revel and ungodly glee' (I, 2, 14–15). While the roving adventures of a lonely hero can be located in the romance tradition, the focus on inner states of turmoil and passion testify to the Romantic nature of this hero:

> I *have* thought
> Too long and darkly, till my brain became,
> In its own eddy boiling and o'erwrought,
> A whirling gulf of fantasy and flame:
>
> (III, 7, 55–8)

The wild natural images, internalised as a sign of tormented consciousness, give force to the sense of individual dislocation. In other uses of medieval settings, historical and poetic distance provides the mysterious atmosphere for the discussion of love and passion. Coleridge's 'Christabel' (1816), following the patterns of eighteenth-century imitations of feudal romances, is set in a world of knights, ladies, honour and portentous dreams. In a similar vein, in Keats's 'Eve of St Agnes' (1820), the superstitions associated with the chivalric world give an air of mystery to the tale of illicit love.

In contrast, the popular Romanticism of Sir Walter Scott domesticates or assimilates romance forms, settings and adventures within the bounds of his present. He employs less extravagant or dramatic features from the Gothic romance. Influenced by eighteenth-century antiquarianism and the romance tradition, Scott's novels use familiarly Gothic environments, highly appropriate to the Scottish settings and imbued with Scottish folklore and history. In *The Bride of Lammermoor* (1819), the spectral return of a past family horror is implicated in fierce clan rivalries. The romance tradition is used with a degree of ironic detachment: the past and its Gothic trappings provide the background for romanticised adventures of warriors, pirates and lovers, adventures that are often used self-consciously as signs of youthful enchantment and folly. The hero of Scott's *Waverley* (1814) is in this mould: steeped in romances, his love of adventure is presented in a lightly quixotic manner as the amusing *naïveté* of a young dreamer. Romances thus provide a way of modifying the eighteenth-century novel of manners and morals by flavouring it with the charms of adventure and superstition that are kept at a distance from the bourgeois values of professionalism, industry and legality in the present. Scott tames the excesses of Gothic romance by assimilating it within acceptable literary bounds.

Scott, more enamoured of the antiquarian aspect of the romance revival, nonetheless enjoyed Gothic fiction, and was one of the few reviewers who approved of Mary Shelley's *Frankenstein* (1818). For Scott, writing in *Blackwood's Edinburgh Magazine* (1818), the novel used marvellous incident to enquire into the conditions and implications of human knowledge and imagination. Other critics, like the reviewer for the *Edinburgh (Scot's) Magazine* (1818), deprecated the evident Godwinian influence in its lack of piety, its 'monstrous conceptions' marking the consequences of 'the wild and irregular theories of the age' (p. 253). He also noted, in its 'dark and gloomy views of nature and man' (p. 249), a distinctly unwelcome version of Gothic writing. *Frankenstein*, though one of the texts now synomymous with Gothic, deploys standard Gothic conventions sparingly to bring the genre thoroughly and critically within the orbit of Romanticism. Its villain is also the hero and victim, while diabolical agency has been replaced by human, natural and scientific powers. Pervaded by the political, philosophical, aesthetic and scientific issues of its time and set in the eighteenth rather than the fifteenth century, the novel has few, though important, traces of older Gothic elements: ruined castles only appear, significantly, in the distance, perched on rocky outcrops and lost in the more important romantic scenery of mountains. Graveyards and charnel houses appear briefly to signal the horror of Frankenstein's enterprise and associate it with the work of necromancers. It is later, in the 1831 introduction to the novel, that Mary Shelley offers another Gothic frame in her account of readings from *Fantasmagoriana*, a French translation of a German collection of tales published in Paris in 1812 and, with a new title – *Tales of the Dead* (1813), in England a year later. These stories led to the ghost story competition held between Byron, Shelley, Polidori and herself.

The belated introduction inscribes another frame around a novel composed of frames. Using different first-person narrators and collecting various stories and letters, the novel alludes to the complexity and mystery of Gothic narratives. With the silent reader presented on the margins of the text as the addressee of the letters that compose the novel, the figure of the eighteenth-century reader is invoked. These features do not close the novel in a conventionally moral manner, but produce a distance from the different figures in the tale to leave a sense of uncertainty and irresolution. Fragmented, disunified, assembled from bits and pieces, the novel is like the monster itself, and like the unnatural, disproportionate monsters of Gothic romances. The monster is also a political figure, an allusion to the monsters that proliferated in the debates concerning the French Revolution, debates in which Mary Shelley's parents, Godwin and Mary Wollstonecraft, took an active part. A metaphor of the violent mob loosed in times of political upheaval, the monster, in the powerful critique he enunciates of human social and political institutions, also represents a radicalism too disturbing to be countenanced by the existing order and which, in the manner of *Caleb Williams*, highlights the monstrosity of systems of law, religion and family.

The most striking scene of the novel, replayed and rewritten in many films, is its moment of creation, a moment that has become the most enduring aspect of the tale's mythological dimensions. Signalling the effects of human aspirations for natural and physical powers beyond the limits of humanity, the monster has come to represent the fears about the existence of both natural and artifical mechanisms that not only exceed the boundaries of a humanised world but emerge, transgressively and destructively, from un-controllable desires and imaginings in the individual mind. The scientific replacement of nature and humanity, the various means of producing and reproducing the material world and the creation of entities that threaten human existence, is a recurrent horror, undermining the naturalness and stability of any order of identity or society.

Frankenstein is not just a scientist in the modern empirical sense. His project is imbued with the grander speculations of alchemical power, speculations which, in the context of natural philosophy, promise, not supernatural knowledge, but the awesome secrets of nature, the mind and the body in the manner laid out by chemical and electrical experiments of the time. In the attempt to deliver life in full and forever, Frankenstein delivers a humanist dream, associated as much with poetic as with scientific imagination. As a dream, an aesthetic as much as scientific enterprise that is horribly realised, it is reflected, in the novel, in the shadow of the monster, a figure both natural and unnatural, living and dead, human and inhuman. Though Frankenstein descends into a world dominated by the monster, violently raving in his destructive pursuit of his abortive creation, the novel does not present this as a simple case of delusion or madness. The monster is not simply an *alter ego* of Frankenstein, not simply the passionate returning of the repressed energies of a deranged individual mind. For, attending to psychological details, the novel presents the monster as both a private and public horror: he has an autonomous existence manifested by his eloquence and critical intelligence and in the effects he has on others.

This is underlined by the patterns of doubling and reversal in the novel. The first narrator, Walton, is an explorer, possessed of dreams to discover the North Pole and its secrets of magnetism, dreams that are akin to Frankenstein's in that they envisage a world of eternal light. His sympathy, on meeting Frankenstein, also signals that they double each other. The process of doubling is extended in the figure of Clerval who dreams of learning Eastern languages in order to participate in the colonial commercial exploitation of the East, an enterprise analogous to Walton's hopes of entering a new northern land and Frankenstein's wresting of the secret of life from a feminised Nature. The exclusive and totalising ambition of these projects is encapsulated by Frankenstein's statement that he intends to transcend the bounds of life and death, flood the world with light and create a 'new species' that will adore him like a father. Assembling a creature designed to be beautiful he is repulsed at its ugliness when animated by the spark of life. His vivid nightmare signals the total reversal of his project: images of death, decay, sexuality and woman return, like the monster, to haunt him with the antithesis and consequence of his idealist fantasy. The total and absolutely unified vision that animated his project, a vision in which self predominates, is reversed and shown to be dependent on the figures of difference it tried to negate. Frankenstein's subjectivity disintegrates, its imagined and vain sovereignty turning into the passions and violence of a Gothic villain: creation cedes to destruction, mastery to slavery, unity to monstrosity.

While the doublings and reversals suggest a critique of the Gothic implications of the distinctly masculine Romantic imagination, of a humanism grown monstrous as a result of excessive and exclusive aspirations to power and ideal unity, the novel, while presenting the destructive effects on family, gender and social relations, does not end with either an affirmation of domestic values or a moral reprimand. Monstrosity has left the novel open, its frames broken: all boundaries are left in question, divided between the positions of Frankenstein and the monster. The creator dies, the monster disappears in darkness and distance, while Walton, having agreed to return home, still gazes towards the Pole. Home and domestic values, after the early descriptions of Frankenstein's ideal upbringing in a republican and bourgeois Genevan family, are rendered suspect. Moral and legal systems, too, are tainted by monstrosity in the trial and execution of an innocent woman. As a result another woman, Frankenstein's fiancé Elizabeth, comments on a horror that pervades the novel: that all distinctions have irrevocably collapsed, that nothing is certain or grounded but teeters on the brink of an abyss (p. 93). It is on a similar brink that the novel ends, divided by a monstrous transgression that is doubled, both internal and external, embedded in psychological and social forms, leaving all boundaries uncertain, delivered to a horrified glimpse of movements and powers shaping identity but beyond any human control.

Exceeding any authorial control, *Frankenstein* crossed generic boundaries to disseminate in popular culture and modern mythology as a byword for horror. First staged in 1823, in Richard Brinsley Peake's *Presumption; or the Fate of Frankenstein*, the novel was dramatised, in burlesque and melodramatic forms, fifteen times by 1826. The theatre was important in the process of popularising Gothic terrors and horrors and often framed texts with new, and often more acceptable, meanings, as the title of Peake's production of Frankenstein indicates. The melodramatic and sensational aspects of Gothic fiction were also suited to the stage, and many novelists, Lewis and Walpole included, wrote plays. Another writer of novels and dramas was the Irish clergyman Charles Robert Maturin, whose *Bertram* (1816) was a popular success. In Gothic terms, however, Maturin's most significant work is the perplexing and tortuous *Melmoth the Wanderer* (1820), often considered the last truly Gothic text.

WANDERERS AND DOUBLES

In the dedication to *The Milesian Chief* (1812), Maturin describes his literary talent as the Gothic capacity 'of darkening and gloomy, and of deepening the sad; of painting life in extremes, and representing those struggles of passion when the soul trembles on the verge of the unlawful and unhallowed'. He goes on to describe an earlier novel, *Fatal Revenge* (1807), as an exploration of the 'ground forbidden to man; the sources of visionary terror; the "formless and the void"'. In *The Milesian Chief* he says he has tried 'the equally obscure recesses of the human heart' (pp. iv–vi). The examination of similar Gothic extremes, with particular emphasis on psychological horror and human evil, is continued in *Melmoth*. Appearing, as a contributor to the *Monthly Review* (xciv, 1821) observed, at a time when, 'overwhelmed by their own extravagance', Gothic novels were in decline, the novel revives 'the predilection for impossibility', and 'the passion for the violent, ferocious, and dreadful in poetry' (pp. 81–90).

The novel is also compared to the works of Radcliffe and Godwin, a combination that describes its generic strangeness, its belated use of characteristically eighteenth-century Gothic machinery alongside agonised outcasts and psychological horrors. *Melmoth*'s extensive and intertwined narratives describe terrible and fantastic adventures that traverse Ireland, England, Spain and Indian islands. Horrors are encountered among ruined churches, in stormy and desolate landscapes and in the subterranean passages, burial vaults and prisons of Catholic monasteries. Mob violence, domestic tyranny, seduction and various forms of oppression are documented in Gothic terms. The narrative frame, a manuscript telling of an obscure family past and reinforced by a portrait that seems strangely alive, refers back to classical Gothic devices. Catholicism and its Holy Inquisition, associated by Gothic convention with tyranny, injustice and superstition, is strongly attacked by Maturin, a Protestant cleric in Catholic

Ireland. Other religious doctrines, even the Calvinism to which Maturin adhered, are implicated in general criticisms which blur doctrinal distinctions in the ambiguous malevolence of the Wanderer. Ambiguous, like the novel, Melmoth is drawn from the models of Radcliffean villain and Godwinian Romantic outcast. His malevolence, violent rages, despotic power and blazing eyes are similar to the characteristics of Racliffe's Montoni, but, in contrast, Melmoth is not a mortal made supernaturally diabolical by superstitious imagination: he does possess superhuman capabilities of longevity and magical powers of movement. Melmoth literalises the ghostly and diabolical powers that are only imagined by Radcliffe's heroines.

Though described in religious terms as satanic throughout the course of the novel, Melmoth appears as a spectral double of the human, his image and story emerging gradually from the stories of his many victims. He disavows his satanic role, appearing more like a tempter who preys upon human desperation and desire. The evil he discloses is distinctly, intrinsically, human rather than externally diabolical: 'Enemy of mankind!', Melmoth exclaims, ' . . . how absurdly is that title bestowed on the great angelic chief . . . what enemy has man so deadly as himself' (p. 436). Evil has a banal, human existence, produced from accidents and circumstance to escalate beyond human control. Melmoth's criticisms of religious tyranny also encompass the mundane absurdities, perversities and corruptions of human passions, vanities and social habits.

Much of the drama in *Melmoth* is internalised in details of horror, suffering and anguish. Melmoth is also a victim, like Caleb or Falkland. A Faustian figure, like St Leon, he sells his soul for knowledge and power, to become a Cain figure, a Wandering Jew, an outcast and a rebel. A cursed wanderer, he will only be free to die if another takes his place, exchanging his powers and cursed condition for their sufferings of which he is not the cause: everyday life and the corruption of social and religious institutions take care of that. The persecution and torment caused by these institutions is detailed in the novel's many accounts of alienation, desperation and mental deterioration. One sufferer, Moncada, describes the psychological effects of monastic imprisonment as 'something like the conspiracies so often occurring in the convent . . . an attempt to involve me in some plot against myself, something in which I might be led to be active in my own condemnation' (pp. 231–2). Such paranoia, and the delusional loss of any sense of self and reality that it entails, is not, however, enough for him to be seduced by Melmoth's offers of freedom.

Melmoth is a particularly unsuccessful tempter, a victory perhaps for the personal faith engendered by the Reformation. That faith remains a bleak hope in a novel in which physical and psychological torment constitutes the only basis for human reality and dignity: 'while people think it worth their while to torment us, we are never without some dignity' (p. 251). Humanity, communication and feeling tenuously emerge as effects of suffering, betrayal, disillusion and guilt, an inevitable condition emphasised by the form of the novel. The complexity, the confusing density of the narrative frames, do not, like conventional Gothic texts, restore a moral order or explain a mystery, but suggest that the human condition is as inescapable as the narrative labyrinth itself, a relentless chain of cruel events without purpose, unity or meaning. In this respect the novel performs an ironic reversal of romance ideals and their homogenising effects.

'Reality' is repeatedly contrasted with Gothic fictions. During the relation of one characteristically Gothic adventure romances are described as habituating readers to 'tales of subterranean passages, and supernatural horrors' but failing to represent the real 'breathless horror felt by a being engaged in an enterprise beyond his powers, experience, or calculation, driven to trust his life and liberation to hands that reeked with a father's blood' (p. 191). Reality and fiction are not clearly separated, but are tortuously entwined in this self-conscious twisting of distinctions that appears at once serious and silly. Romance distinctions are undercut by challenges to readers' expectations, like the comments on Isidora's display of anxiety and terror in a situation all too common to a romance heroine. The grandeur of Gothic terrors is steadily and comically undercut by the absorption of Gothic horrors into the banal and everyday world:

> Romances have been written and read, whose interest arose from the noble and impossible defiance of the heroine to all powers human and superhuman alike. But neither the writers or readers seem ever to have taken into account the thousand petty external causes that operate on human agency with a force, if not more powerful, far more effective than the grand internal motive which makes so grand a figure in romance, and so rare and trivial a one in common life.

(p. 372)

The internalisation of grand Gothic devices is ambivalently externalised, diffused throughout an everyday world itself composed of fictions. Maturin's disturbing reflections render reality in part an effect of fictions, and yet worse, not better, than Gothic terrors. Grand romantic aspirations, internalised and reproduced in social and generic codes and fictions, are inverted as superstitious misconceptions: horror is banal in origin, an inescapable reality, internal to the workings of the everyday and the subjects of circumstance who inhabit it. *Melmoth* becomes an anti-romance in contesting the purgative functions of terror that externalise and aggrandise quotidian evils. Art, life and horror are tortuously intertwined in a vicious play that refuses distinctions of fiction and reality: 'there was no luxury of inventive art to flatter the senses, or ennervate the attention, – to enable the hearer to break the spell that binds him to the world of horrors, and recover the soothing realities and comforts of ordinary life . . . ' (p. 398). Maturin's fiction offers no conventional novelistic escape and recuperation of reality, only the pervasively literal horrors of a world painted in Gothic colours. The interrelation of fiction and reality, internal and external worlds of horror, of irreconcilable conflicts and warring extremes, for Maturin, is characterised by Ireland: 'the only country on earth, where, from the strange existing opposition of religion, politics, and manners, the extremes of refinement and barbarism are united, and the most wild and incredible situations of romantic story are hourly passing before modern eyes' (dedication to *The Milesian Chief*, p. v). Gothic romance again transcribes and displaces anxieties and horrors in the everyday.

The Gothic nature of Maturin's Ireland is not unique. Scott's novels present his native Scotland as wild and romantic and thus appropriately Gothic settings. James Hogg's *The Private Memoirs and Confessions of a Justified Sinner* (1824) also uses the Scottish context to good Gothic effect. While Maturin coloured the world in the dark hues of Gothic fiction, Hogg's novel focuses on a similar collision of extremes in an individual psyche. In the *Memoirs*, too, religious ideas – Calvinism, Presbyterianism and antinomianism – predominate among scenes of Scottish political conflicts between prelatic and covenanter mobs. From the social context and descriptions of the political and familial conflict and the strict religious environment in which the protagonist is brought up, an increasingly disarming world of delusion and uncertainty emerges. An 'editor's' narrative explains events as the fratricidal and cunning crimes of a man determined to inherit the family wealth that has been denied him from birth. There are, however, some mysterious events, especially the appearance of a dark stranger, that allude to supernatural machinations. In the subsequent confessional account by the criminally Cain-like brother, Robert Wringhim, the boundaries of social and subjective reality are utterly disturbed. Wringhim, raised by a local Reverend instead of his aristocratic family, is taught that, as one of the Elect, his place in Heaven is secure, no matter what he does on earth. Meeting a stranger capable of transforming his physical appearance, Robert is encouraged in crime, initially haunting his brother, George Colwan, before luring him into a duel in which the latter is stabbed in the back. Taking possession of the Colwan estates, Robert discovers he has indulged in bouts of drinking, love affairs and business deals of which he has no recollection. He speculates that a 'second self', his own likeness, or some spirit possessing his body, is responsible: it is never clear whether these are excuses for evil, figures of unconscious forces, temporary lapses of sanity or effects of diabolical agency. The strange double, execrated in Gothic terms as a 'monster of nature' and a 'devil incarnate' (p. 189), persecutes Wringhim to the extent that, psychologically and physically wretched, he is tortured by terrible voices and hideous, nightmarish fiends, no longer possessed of any sense of self, nor daring to look in a mirror 'for I shuddered at my own image and likeness' (p. 205). The image, like his double, only exacerbates his alienation, misery and self-loathing. In a world of fantastic images and distorting doubles, he can only be divided from himself, drawn in by their lure, an image, a semblance, 'liker to a vision than a human being' (p. 216).

Framed by an editorial account of events using eye-witness reports, journal evidence and even an article by a writer named Hogg, the confessions are held at a distance as the autobiographical ravings of a madman. The editorial frame ironically plays with Gothic devices aimed at verisimilitude and, after trying to assess the authenticity of the confessions and their significance as allegory or parable, the 'editor' offers other possibilities: 'In short we must either conceive him not only the greatest fool, but the greatest wretch, on whom was ever stamped the form of humanity; or, that he was a religious maniac, who wrote and wrote about a deluded creature, till he arrived at that height of madness that he believed himself the very object whom he had been all along describing' (pp. 229–30). An ironic comment on the identifications and doublings of Romantic and Gothic writing, this suspicious recognition of writing's uncanny powers and reading's strange effects is made after the events comprising the story have been written twice. The *Memoirs*, it seems, is similarly doubled, ambivalently negotiating between two forms of narrative in a process that repeats Gothic dynamics of internalisation and externalisation.

The *Memoirs'* ironic distance manages to sustain a distinction between internal and external worlds even as it acknowledges the curious, ambivalent effects of writing's duplicity. Its fascination with delusion and psychological disturbance maintains an individual case as its object. The fascination with deranged states and uncanny experiences, uncertainly imagined or horribly real, recurs throughout later Gothic fiction in attempts to represent these conditions subjectively or objectively. The different narratives of Hogg's novel perform both strategies, one looking at mental deterioration from the inside, the other from the outside. Both these angles are explored in nineteenth-century renderings of the uncanny: they are internally presented with the attention on doubles and mirrors, and externally objectified as cases of criminal or psychological degeneration. Between the two, the status of human identity, social forms and Gothic styles underwent significant changes in location and significance.

6

HOMELY GOTHIC

In general we are reminded that the word *'heimlich'* is not
unambiguous, but belongs to two sets of ideas, which,
without being contradictory, are yet very different: on the one
hand it means what is familiar and agreeable, and on the other,
what is concealed and kept out of sight . . . everything is
unheimlich that ought to have remained secret and hidden but
has come to light.

(Sigmund Freud, 'The Uncanny', pp. 224–5)

In the mid-nineteenth century there is a significant diffusion of
Gothic traces throughout literary and popular fiction, within the
forms of realism, sensation novels and ghost stories especially.
Eighteenth-century Gothic machinery and the wild landscapes of
Romantic individualism give way to terrors and horrors that are
much closer to home, uncanny disruptions of the boundaries
between inside and outside, reality and delusion, propriety and
corruption, materialism and spirituality. These are signified by the
play of ghosts, doubles and mirrors. In both American and British
writing the influence of Radcliffe, Godwin and Scott is still
evident, though their Gothic styles are significantly transformed.

The bourgeois family is the scene of ghostly return, where guilty secrets of past transgression and uncertain class origins are the sources of anxiety. The modern city, industrial, gloomy and labyrinthine, is the locus of horror, violence and corruption. Scientific discoveries provide the instruments of terror, and crime and the criminal mind present new threatening figures of social and individual disintegration. The traces of Gothic and Romantic forms, however, appear as signs of loss and nostalgia, projections of a culture possessed of an increasingly disturbing sense of deteriorating identity, order and spirit.

The development of the American novel owes much to the reception and transformation of European romantic literature. Significant differences appear in the use of Gothic images in writing that was predominantly realist. Hackneyed Gothic machinery was abandoned, but contrasts of light and dark, good and evil, were inflected in texts in which the mysteries of the mind or of family pasts were the central interest: the human and social world completely replaced the grand Gothic terrors of a supernatural kind. In the American context a different geography and history were available to writers: romantic adventures could take place in the wilds of an uncharted continent or horrors could be found in the Puritan witch trials of Salem in the seventeenth century. Gothic psychology and the questions narratives raise of the reality of strange incidents are framed with different issues: of rationalism, democracy and religious organisation, and their relationship to individual freedom and social control.

The malevolent aristocrats, ruined castles and abbeys and chivalric codes dominating a gloomy and Gothic European tradition were highly inappropriate to the new world of North America. They were too far removed to have the same significance or effects of terror. As Nathaniel Hawthorne, in the preface to *The Marble Faun* (1860), rather optimistically observed: 'No author without a trial, can conceive of the difficulty of writing a romance about a country where there is no shadow, no mystery, no picturesque and gloomy wrong, nor anything but commonplace prosperity, in broad and simple daylight, as is happily the case with my dear native land' (pp. x–xi). In Hawthorne's earlier novels there were many peculiarly American shadows that fell upon the 'broad and simple daylight' of American life. Though the grand gloom of European Gothic was inappropriate, the commonplace of American culture was full of little mysteries and guilty secrets from communal and family pasts. In 1865 Henry James, who wrote many ghost stories later in the century, criticised, in an essay on the sensation novelists Mary Braddon and Wilkie Collins, Radcliffe's external and extravagant sources of excitement, when, more interesting and terrible, were the strangenesses closer to home. James states that a good ghost-story 'must be connected at a hundred points with the common objects of life' (p. 742). The newness of the American world, however, retained some shadows of superstitious fancy which appeared in concerns with the relation of the individual, mentally and politically, to social and religious forms of order. The negotiation with fictions of the past, as both a perpetuation and disavowal of superstitious fears and habits, attempts to banish certain shadows haunting the American daylight and discovers new dark shapes.

AMERICAN GOTHIC: BROWN, HAWTHORNE, POE

Charles Brockden Brown, the first native-born American professional writer, occupies an important position in regard to transformations in Gothic writing. Negotiating European and American Gothic traditions, he was one of the Shelleys' favourite writers. Brown's novels drew on Godwin's fiction and philosophy but adapted themes of persecution, criminality and social tyranny as well as Enlightenment notions of freedom and democracy. Mystery underwent a similar transformation: psychological motivations and delusions were examined in relation to their social and aesthetic implications. Between 1798 and 1800 Brown published four novels concerned with persecution, murder and the powers and terrors of the human mind. *Wieland*, his first, describes the life of two orphans, Clara and Theodore Wieland, growing up in the context of religious evangelism and enlightened rationality. A balance between these two discourses appears to be sustained until the sound of strange voices disrupts the community. Wieland interprets these voices as emanations from God. It is, however, his devout faith that leads to the horrors that destroy the community: believing it to be God's will, Wieland kills his wife, children and himself.

The strange occurrences are subsequently explained in the memoirs appended to the novel as the effects of a human *diabolus ex machina*. The memoirs tell the story of Carwin, a 'biloquist' or ventriloquist able to throw his voice and perfectly imitate the voices of others. His talent makes him an outcast and, after years of wandering and persecution, he settles near the Wieland's community to haunt its members with his biloquistic skills. What is never explained or confessed is Carwin's involvement in Wieland's crimes, whether he urged their commission or whether they really were the result of a deluded religious imagination. The interweaving of distinct tales that link *Wieland* to the Gothic romance also underlines its different perspective on the nature of the mysterious. Mysteries are located in the empirical world, in the natural powers of Carwin and in the chain of events that lead to crime. The implication of the two tales, and the way key issues are left uncertain, disclose a greater realm of mystery in the complexity of motivations and fantasies that determine and delude individual behaviour. Rational explanation of natural powers and its mechanistic image of a universe beyond human control shifts the realm of mystery from a Gothic netherworld of supernatural agency to a physical and empirical world. But the force of delusion inspired by religious devotion still remains somewhat mysterious and inexplicable, and presents, not the victory of enlightenment, but a new and different darkness.

The uncertain relation between religion and rationalism is, in *Wieland*, located at the level of political and aesthetic representation. The ambivalence, like that of Gothic concerns with the dangerous effects of imagination and novel-reading, is not resolved. In the American context the ambivalence reflects an anxiety about the constitution of American society itself. In part demystifying European Gothic traditions of superstitious and aristocratic terror, and in part relocating their mystery from the supernatural to a human and natural sphere, *Wieland* refuses the dichotomy of religious mysticism and enlightened rationalism: it casts suspicion on the authority and effects of their representations and identifies the shadows that fall as a result of the lights of either reason or revelation. Moreover, it is a darkness suggestive of individual pathology and an effect of the repressions and desires produced by authoritative representations.

Nathaniel Hawthorne's engagement with romance, in contrast to Brockden Brown's, departs in the direction of realism. Less concerned with criminality and individual psychopathology, Hawthorne demystifies Gothic representations of a haunting past and associated superstitions lingering in the present to look at the play of sunshine and shadow in family and society. In *The Scarlett Letter* (1850) the spectre of Puritan intolerance and witchcraft trials hangs over the community that condemns a young woman, Hester, to wear a large red 'A' as a mark of her adultery. Demonised, Hester and her child live defiantly as outcasts on the fringes of the community. The child's father lives a guilty and anxious life in the community, wearing a veneer of respectability that becomes increasingly thin, as thin as the line separating good from evil. The boundaries and conventions distinguishing good from bad are, in the exclusions they legitimate and the repressions they demand, as much a site of darkness and uncertainty as Hester's 'immorality'.

While *The Scarlet Letter* focuses on the limits of social propriety, other Hawthorne stories imbue the past with more psychological interest. In 'Young Goodman Brown' (1835), a young man's nocturnal journey into a forest at night leads to an encounter with respected churchgoers and elders. His mysterious companion suggests that they are not the shining examples of propriety that they appear to be. Arriving at a witches' sabbath Goodman Brown discovers a social spectrum of supposedly respectable as well as disreputable figures. The short story ends on an uncertain note, unable to decide whether the events were dreamt or real, whether they were the deluded visions of a superstitious young man or the dark side of the community as a whole. One thing is sure: the diabolical effects of the account itself. Brown returns a changed man to an apparently unchanged community: he is deeply suspicious of all outward appearances and all forms of faith, distrustful and gloomy until his dying day.

The play of appearances, of past and present, superstition and reality, remains in the lighter tones of Hawthorne's second novel, *The House of the Seven Gables* (1851). As in conventional Gothic texts, it centres on a building. Not an old castle or mansion, Hawthorne's edifice is a family house. Like a Gothic castle, however, it is a gloomy and grotesquely ornamented repository of ghosts. Harking back to the early days of American colonisation, the story centres on the theft of the land on which the house was built. The victim, Maule, curses Pyncheon, the new owner. The latter dies shortly afterwards, establishing the basis for local superstition. Two generations later, the family is in decline and, like ghosts, haunting rather than inhabiting the house and its memories of transgression. The arrival of a stranger, a young daguerrotypist, and the death of the senior member of the family in the same manner as the grandfather precipitate a very Gothic conclusion. The stranger, the heir of old Maule, reclaims the property by marrying the youngest member of the Pyncheon family. Because he knows past secrets about the house, he also finds the deeds entitling him to great estates. These have been hidden in the house for years. The ghosts are thus purged: replaced by the values of property and domesticity. Mysteries are explained, the deaths resulting, not from the curse, but from apoplexy. Superstitions linger in the reaction to more modern features. Old Gothic portraits are superseded by daguerrotype photography, demonic possession by the science of mesmerism. While the present excises the superstitions of the past and domesticates Gothic terrors, daguerrotype representations have uncanny effects in bringing the dead to life, until, that is, the picture is revealed to be of a living rather than dead relative.

The uncanny effects of representation are addressed elsewhere by Hawthorne in stories dealing with artistic creation. In 'The Artist of the Beautiful' ([1844] 1987) a clockmaker labours for years to replicate perfectly a flying butterfly only to have his successful mechanical wonder destroyed by the clumsy grasp of a child. The production of beauty is not an idealised enterprise in Hawthorne for it involves obsessive and wearying labour that undermines a sense of reality. The lures of beauty are presented in the Hoffmanesque fantasy 'Rappacini's Daughter' ([1844] 1987). E. T. A Hoffman, the German Romantic writer of marvellous and ghostly tales was a strong influence on Hawthorne and Poe. Stories like 'The Golden Pot' ([1814] 1992) describe fantastic, dream-like worlds full of magical events and exotic imagery while others, like 'The Sand-Man' ([1815] 1992), describe an individual's descent into states of delusion and insanity. In 'Rappacini's Daughter' both the daughter of the reclusive professor, Rappacini, and his marvellous garden of exotic plants are extremely attractive and lethally poisonous, their allure drawing a young man to the brink of death. The world of artifice and representation is seen to possess mysterious powers in the stimulation of fantasy and hallucination.

The distortions of the imagination are best presented in the macabre, hallucinatory stories of Edgar Allan Poe. In Poe's tales and stories the outward trappings of eighteenth-century Gothic, the gloom, decay and extravagance, are, in chilling and terrific evocations, turned inward to present psychodramas of diseased imaginings and deluded visions that take grotesque fantasies to spectral extremes. The horror in Poe's tales exhibits a morbid fascination with darkly exotic settings mirroring extreme states of disturbed consciousness and imaginative excess, presenting fatal beauties, bloody hauntings, premature entombment and ghastly metempsychosis. Human desires and neuroses are dressed in the lurid hues of the supernatural to the extent that nightmare and reality become entwined.

Poe's extensive reading in the works of British and German Gothic writers shapes his ambivalent attitude to the genre. Aware of the humorous possibilities of the formulaic Gothic tales popularised in periodicals like *Blackwood's Magazine*, and the ironies inherent in Romanticism and outlined by August Schlegel, one of his favourite authors along with the novelist and dramatist Ludwig Tieck, Poe's tales sustain a distance, an ambivalence towards the terrors and imaginings they present.

Questioning as well as promoting the dark powers of the imagination, Poe's fiction leaves boundaries between reality, illusion and madness unresolved rather than, in the manner of his contemporaries, domesticating Gothic motifs or rationalising mysteries. His subjects are varied, exploring particularly individual cases of delusion and more general anxieties about death. Doubles and mirrors are used to splendid effect, while scientific theories are employed to present natural sources of horror in which detection uncovers criminal rather than supernatural mysteries.

In 'William Wilson', first published in 1839 (1967), Poe's schooldays in England are recalled in a story that has all the architectural and atmospheric trappings of earlier Gothic. The tale of a boy encountering another of the same name who infuriates him by means of vocal and sartorial imitation, 'William Wilson' exploits the theme of doubling, but without the distancing effects of the editorial frame used by Hogg in his *Memoirs*. The hero of the tale leads a dissolute life, but finds, wherever he travels, his illegitimate schemes thwarted by the figure that haunted him at school. He finally locks his double in a duel, to find, on running his opponent through, that he is alone and bleeding before a great mirror: his mortal foe has been his inverted image, an *alter ego* that, unlike the *doppelgänger*, is a better self, an external image of good conscience. The climax turns the tale around: what appeared to be an account of some external haunting is seen as the subjective distortions of a hallucinating individual. In 'The Fall of the House of Usher' ([1834] 1967), boundaries between consciousness and reality are more uncertain than the fatal delusions of 'William Wilson'. The house is both a Gothic manifestation, an architectural ruin set in a desolate and gloomy landscape and a family equally in decay, dying from an unknown and incurable disease. A friend arrives to witness the family's demise, seeing, in an atmosphere of attentuated sensibility, the sister and brother gradually fade into shadows. The luxurious and languid decline is punctuated by a shocking Gothic climax. On the point of death, the brother announces that his sister has been buried alive. Suddenly secret panels slide back to reveal the enshrouded form of the sister who falls upon her brother in a mutual moment of death. Rather than ponder the erotic implications of this macabrely shocking moment, the narrator flees as storms gather and the house itself crashes in utter ruin. The imagination, suspended and tortured in this gloomy and unreal world, reaches its own collapse.

The morbid and macabre images of premature burial and the return of the dead are given a more human and more realistic twist in 'The Cask of Amontillado' ([1846] 1967). Premature burial constitutes the climactic horror of a tale of chillingly executed vengeance. Preying upon the weakness of an old enemy – his pride in his knowledge of wine – the narrator relates how he is enticed into vaults to taste an uncertain vintage. The narrator then relates how he enchained his victim and then walled him within a recess deep in the vaults. More horrible still are the self-satisfied tones of the narrator. The vaults lend a Gothic atmosphere to what is essentially a horror story about a callously inhuman intelligence.

In other stories, like 'Ligeia' ([1838] 1967), the grotesque scenery and descriptions of the ghostly return of a loved, dead wife are the external reflections of an imagination decayed by loss and opium addiction. Crime, in 'The Tell-Tale Heart' ([1843] 1967), is treated with a similar ambivalence concerning subjective and objective phenonema: a murderer is driven to confess his crime by the pounding assumed to be the heart of his victim's body concealed beneath the floorboards. In 'The Facts in the Strange Case of Mr Valdemar' ([1845] 1967), contemporary scientific themes provide the basis for a more metaphysical exploration of the horror attendant on disturbances of the boundaries between life and death. In the tale, the mesmerising of a dying man leaves him in a state of suspended animation: the body does not decay but it, or something, can speak, uttering the impossible words 'I am dead'. This statement confounds distinctions between life and death as they are maintained by linguistic conventions, indicating the fragility of the boundaries of nature that are manipulated by the scientific imagination. The horror surrounding the question of who or what is speaking is followed by the release of the body from mesmeric limbo and its speedy decomposition into a liquid mass.

Throughout the tales, the lurid settings and extravagant scenes raise, often playfully, questions about the nature and effects of representation. 'The Oval Portrait' ([1845] 1967), a very short story self-consciously using conventional Gothic devices like the old castle, the life-like portrait and discovered manuscript, discusses representation's capacity to reverse the relationship of life and death: the life-like portrait is a perfect representation of the beautiful love of the artist, completed precisely at the moment the original died. Art, it seems, sucks the life out of things, doubling nature with a disturbing imaginative power, a macabre power of death that recurs throughout all Poe's tales. It is not only the morbid fascination and macabre auras that make them interesting as Gothic works. The various devices, styles and subjects that Poe uses and transforms influence all of subsequent Gothic writing: the doubles, mirrors and the concern with modes of representation; the scientific transgressions of accepted limits; the play of internal and external narrations, of uncertain psychological states and uncanny events; and the location of mysteries in a criminal world to be penetrated by the incisive reason of a new hero, the detective, have become staples of the Gothic.

CITIES, HOMES AND GHOSTS

In Britain in the mid-nineteenth century, Gothic writing was less discernible, having been dispersed among a number of other genres. Ghost stories and sensation novels, shaped by earlier Gothic texts, were popular sources of terror and horror. Though the influence of Scott, Radcliffe and Godwin was evident, significant transformations were made, reflecting the different concerns of the time. A major shift, as in North America, was evident in the domestication of Gothic styles and devices within realistic settings and modes of writing. The architectural and feudal background, the wild landscapes, the aristocratic villains and sentimental heroines, were no longer, in a thoroughly bourgeois culture, objects of terror. Domestic, industrial and urban contexts and aberrant individuals provided the loci for mystery and terror. Haunting pasts were the ghosts of family transgression and guilty concealment; the dark alleyways of cities were the gloomy forests and subterranean labyrinths; criminals were the new villains, cunning, corrupt but thoroughly human. Prisons, social injustice and rebellious individuals were not Romantic sites or heroes of gloomy suffering, but strange figures threatening the home and society. Traditional Gothic traces were strongest in representations of scientific innovation, being associated with alchemy and mystic powers. The lingering dark Romanticism that surrounded accounts of scientific or individual excess was both a threat to social mores and a sign that, in the increasingly normalised and rationalised worlds of family and commerce, there was something missing: a spiritual passion which, in opposition to the more real horrors of everyday corruption, was nostalgically represented in Gothic terms or in the ghost story as a contrast between narrow reality and lost, metaphysical dimensions.

In the popular fiction of the 1830s and 1840s plenty of Gothic and Romantic elements were still used. Edward Bulwer-Lytton's fiction embraced the old romantic forms that he had enjoyed in his youth. A fascination with aristocracy and past ruin is counter-balanced by Godwinian accounts of criminal underworlds, incarceration and individual corruption. The alchemy associated with Godwin's *St Leon* provides the basis of another important strand in Bulwer-Lytton's work, though the latter departs in more arcane directions. A visionary and Romantic mixture of alchemical, Faustian and scientific themes is framed with a mystical idealism that aspires to a suprarational humanism. *Zanoni* (1842) describes the search for metaphysical unity and new dimensions in terms of a hero schooled in occult reading, experimenting in ancient black arts in a search for the *elixir vitae* of the alchemists. In a later, shorter, novel, *The Haunters and the Haunted* (1859), arcane instruments and occult lore are combined with quasi-scientific discussion of energies and fields in a story framed by a sceptical and rational investigator's narrative. The examination of vulgar super-stitions surrounding a supposedly haunted London town house, in order to debunk them, leads the empiricist narrator into an encounter with extremely powerful supernatural forces. Though these are associated with the haunting energies that result from past criminal horrors, they also disclose awful and superhuman secrets: in a secret room the narrator discovers clues to a being possessed of extraordinary mental powers that combine occult and scientific knowledge. These, a later encounter with this being reveals, involve skills in mesmerism as well as inexplicable paranormal abilities and the possession of eternal life. A supermind, the figure that appears in various guises in the story, represents both the desirable peak of Gothic-Romantic imaginings, the total fusion of matter and spirit, and the terrible and threatening implications of such power. While this current of visionary horror lingers throughout the nineteenth century, to resurface strongly at its end, fiction in the middle of the century tended to realise terror and horror, fascinated by their irruption in the shadows of the everyday world.

In the popular romances by William Harrison Ainsworth there is a less visionary blend of Gothic forms that looks at the darkness of crime and the city. His productions were varied, however. In *The Lancashire Witches* (1849), a historical novel beginning with witch trials in the seventeenth century, secret covens and witchcraft rituals are the subject matter. Other novels, involved in the Newgate controversy over fiction that was considered to encourage crime, focus on the villains and their propensity for corrupt and criminal action. In a later novel, *Auriol* (1885), it is the city that is described as a distinctly Gothic scene. Earlier work by G. W. Reynolds also examines this new Gothic scene. Writing supernatural tales with standard Gothic themes, *Faust* (1845–6), *Wagner, the Wehr-Wolf* (1846–7) and *The Necromancer* (1852), Reynolds' darkly realistic work, *Mysteries of London* (1845–8), provides a good example of urban Gothic. Tyranny and horror are both nightmarish and real in its gloomy descriptions of aristocratic corruption and depravity which, in the city's labyrinth of immorality, also enmeshes the behaviour of the working classes. The apparent reality of the city's horrors evokes emotions that ask questions of the social order, emotions relating to fears in the immediate present rather than displaced on to a distant past.

These horrors also influence the Gothic elements of more literary works. Charles Dickens's *Bleak House* (1853) presents a grimly blackened city, while *Oliver Twist* (1838) shows the violence and cruelty lurking just below the surface of acceptable Victorian reality. A great reader of Gothic romances, Dickens deploys their devices in diverse ways and for various effects throughout his fiction, a good example of the dispersal of Gothic elements. In *Great Expectations* (1860–1) aspects of Gothic fantasy, in the shape of Magwitch and Miss Havisham, satirically undercut the aspirations of Pip, who, like superstitious readers of romances, is duped by his own expectations. As creations of distorted imaginings both Pip and Estella are fabricated like Frankenstein's monster. Coketown, in *Hard Times* (1854), is a grimly inhuman industrial labyrinth, a realisation of a distorted and reductive rationalism that has its ideological equivalent represented by the tyranny of numbers and facts which, in Gradgrind's school, are ground into young heads without the spiritually ameliorating influence of any imagination. Traces of Gothic fear and power shadow the bourgeois family and its house in *Little Dorrit* (1855). Having the melancholic and gloomy appearance of the castle, the house and the family within it are haunted by buried secrets of unrespectable origins and the ghostly presence of the father signified by his foreboding portrait.

Dickens was also influential in the growing popularity of another related but distinct genre, the ghost story. Like much Gothic writing in the early part of the nineteenth century, the ghost story was circulated and popularised in literary magazines and periodicals. While the Gothic crossed various historical and natural boundaries in an extravagant fashion, the ghost story's limited encounters with the spectral world focused on the vacillation between real and supernatural dimensions. Generically more contained, the ghost story presents a more definite idea of reality in order to evoke a specifically uncanny effect by the appearance of supernatural figures: as realism's uncanny shadow, the ghost story produces gentle tremors along the line separating the supernatural world from that of Victorian empirical and domestic order. The supernatural is not rationalised, however, but is affirmed as a distinct and unknown presence occupying a narrative that, though incompatible, runs parallel to realist representations. Though incredibly popular throughout the century, the ghost story seemed more a diversion from serious writing. With the exception of the most productive of ghost story writers, Sheridan Le Fanu, who none the less engaged with realism and Gothic forms in his novel, *Uncle Silas* (1864), many of the writers of ghost stories spent more time writing novels along conventional realist lines. In 'The Signalman' (1866), Dickens produced a ghost story of place describing the uncanny recurrence of a tragic event in the same location years later. Mrs Gaskell's 'The Old Nurse's Story' (1852) uses the presence of a child's ghost to disclose a guilty secret in a family's past. In other tales, like Mary Braddon's 'At Chrighton Abbey' ([1871] Cox and Gilbert 1992), the ghost is not only a figure for the past, but returns in spectral anticipation of disaster in the immediate future. The more distant future, too, makes phantom appearances in the present in George Eliot's 'The Lifted Veil' (1859), a tale describing the disarming effects of an individual's extraordinary ability to catch glimpses of the future.

Though affirming, often self-consciously within the tales, the reality of ghostly events, these tales frequently address the question posed in the title of a Mrs Wood story, 'Reality or Delusion?' ([1868] Cox and Gilbert 1992), thus leaving readers uncertain about the story's reality as much as other stories' fictional devices attempt to overcome scepticism and offer convincing supernatural realities. The uncertainty about individual perception and interest in other, supernatural dimensions stimulated by the ghost story, like the more material horrors of social depravity and criminal corruption displayed in Gothic representations of the city, indicate a certain disaffection with the present. Excursions beyond the everyday world, the disturbance of boundaries between present, past and future, indicate both a fear and a nostalgia in relation to Victorian attitudes and society. What is missing, in a thoroughly secular, rationalised and scientifically-ordered material world, the ghost story suggests, is a sense of unity, value and spirit. Ghosts returning from a greater darkness surrounding the culture, as much as the fascination with criminality and social degeneration, signalled this sense of loss.

Gothic and Romantic images were ways of engaging with the alienation from the past as both a repository of the fears of disintegration and the hopes of regaining a sense of unity and value. In Robert Browning's nineteenth-century poetic version of the quest romance, 'Childe Roland to the Dark Tower Came', the bleak landscape and uncertain destination of the wandering hero give form to a cultural sense of spiritual desolation and aimlessness. In Alfred Tennyson's reworking of Arthurian legend, the romantic figures, particularly female as in 'The Lady of Shalott', are identifiable as figures of mourning and separation, their loss mirroring the sense of cultural emptiness that demands a unifying national myth. Romance forms, for some cultural critics, provided a way out of social alienation. John Ruskin's accounts of Gothic architecture uncover a fierceness and strength that, like the freedom and imagination associated with Gothic and romance forms in eighteenth-century antiquarianism, has a vigour and spirit lacking in the soul-destroying and monotonous conditions of Victorian England. An antiquarian angle is pursued by William Morris's use of romances as a utopian and precapitalist alternative to the oppressive forms of industrial capitalism.

SINS OF THE FATHER

The extravagant effects of Gothic and Romantic elements tended, in nineteenth-century fiction, to be refracted through the domestic world central to realism. As the privileged site of Victorian culture, home and family were seen as the last refuge from the sense of loss and the forces threatening social relations. The home, however, could be a prison as well as a refuge. In two novels of the period, novels that engage very differently with Gothic themes, the home is the site of both internal and external pressures, uncanny and terrifying at the same time. In Emily Brontë's *Wuthering Heights*

(1847) Gothic and Romantic forces of individual passion are fearful and invested with a sense of loss. In Wilkie Collins's adaptation of Radcliffean themes in his sensation novel, *The Woman in White* (1860), Gothic terrors are purged from the social and familial world through the determined exercise of rational, legal and investigative powers.

The desolate, stormy and wild landscape and decaying family house of *Wuthering Heights* use Gothic and Romantic elements that, as in Charlotte Brontë's *Jane Eyre* (1847) and *Villette* (1853), signify darker forces of individual passion, natural energy and social restriction. The novel's hero-villain, Heathcliff, combines the roles of Gothic villain and Romantic outcast in his antisocial demeanour, fierce temper, mercenary and unlawful plottings, and his quest for vengeance. With Cathy's rebellious passions, there is a similar refusal of the niceties of domestic passivity, propriety and duty. The narrative structure of reported stories and its uncanny movement between past and present are Gothic elements signalling an untamed and wild invasion of the home rather than comfortable domestication. The Gothic theme that the sins of the father are visited on the offspring is manifested in the representations of the illegitimacy and brutality of paternal authority, the repetition of events, and the doublings of figures and names in successive generations. Earnshaw's domestic tyranny, Hareton's wildness, Linton Heathcliff's unmanliness and Catherine's energy are all displaced duplications of the roles and characteristics of the previous generation. The duplication that signals the dependence of past structures on those of the present is also evident in the dependence of individual identities on those of others. The relationship between Heathcliff and Cathy is the most powerful example of doubling: one constituting the other's narcissistic image of his or her own unified self. The powerful desire for unity, however, disturbs all social and familial relations: Heathcliff's desire demands the transgression of all rules, and casts him in the figure of a fiend, a devil and a vampire. He is also associated with natural wildness, his temperament the mirror of the hostile and stormy environment he occupies.

The distinctions between nature and culture, between individual passions and social rules do not simply distinguish the artificial repressiveness of social forms from the irruption of primitive desires. They are as artificial as the constructions of an originary and natural Gothic world to which they allude, a legacy of eighteenth-century and Romantic distinctions between civilisation and wildness. Heathcliff's passions are produced: he is found in the city and then miserably domesticated by a hostile middle-class family whose criticisms, exclusions and prohibitions of his progress towards the properly bourgeois ends of marriage make him wild and vengeful. Heathcliff represents the outer limit of Romantic individualism, possessed by the desire of an impossible unity invested in the figure of Cathy. If Miss Linton can elope with Heathcliff under the illusion, as the latter scornfully observes, of his romantic heroism, then antithetical characterisations of his wild, untamed nature are similarly illusory constructions signalling the spectral return of Gothic and Romantic forms.

The ghosts of the novel are an effect of the internalisation of a Romantic tradition on a social rather than individual level. Ghosts are not only seen by the narrator Lockwood on his first visit to the Heights, they reappear throughout the text: Heathcliff's is seen with a strange lady by members of the local community. These uncanny effects in the story are, like the effects of the story on Lockwood, signs of the return of a lost world. At the end of the novel the perspective moves from the happy domestic scene at the Heights to Heathcliff's grave. Like a Graveyard poet of the eighteenth century, Lockwood imagines a tranquillity after death, a return to proper unity in the earth. It is a peace that remains imaginary, projections of the beholder's – Lockwood's – sense of loss and his nostalgic dwelling upon the scene: it is as a reader of the story's romantic passions that he has identified with its subject. The text, framed by Lockwood's longing gaze, has constructed a lost natural passion and spirit that is at once strange and desirable as a site of unity.

In *The Woman in White* the transgressions of individual desire threaten family and society from within. Wilkie Collins was pre-eminent among the sensation novelists of the 1860s. Sensational effects, however, owe much to Gothic, particularly Radcliffean, styles of evoking terror, mystery and superstitious expectation. The plot, figures and narrative form of *The Woman in White* also structurally resemble Radcliffe's Gothic, though transposed into shapes more appropriate to the nineteenth century. Henry James, in the *Nation* (1765), credits Collins with 'having introduced into fiction those most mysterious of mysteries, the mysteries which are at our own door'. 'Instead of the terrors of "Udolpho"', James goes on, 'we were treated to the terrors of the cheerful country-house and the busy London lodgings. And there is no doubt that these were infinitely the more terrible' (p. 742). None the less, Gothic patterns pervade Collins's novel. The Gothic heroine, passive and persecuted, is presented as an image of loss and suffering, especially when seen through the eyes of that new Victorian hero, the amateur detective. Anne Catherick, the woman of the title, is scarcely present in the novel, her spectral appearances in dark city streets, deserted graveyards and garden retreats gesturing towards the mysteries and terrors the narrative resolves. As a ghostly figure pointing to the past crimes of an illegitimate aristocrat and the sufferings and persecutions which he inflicts on her, Anne Catherick's appearances also anticipate the trials of the novel's Gothic heroine who, as a half-sister, is both literally and narratively her double. As a reminder of older Gothic family romance patterns, the double is also used to present a more terrible possibility as a figure that threatens the loss of identity.

The novel, indeed, is framed quite self-consciously as a Gothic romance. Towards the end, the hero, Hartright, reviews the story:

'The sins of the father shall be visited on the children.' But for the fatal resemblance between the two daughters of one father,

the conspiracy of which Anne had been the innocent instru-
ment and Laura the innocent victim, could never have been
planned. With what unerring and terrible directness the long
chain of circumstances led down from the thoughtless wrong
committed by the father to the heartless injury inflicted on the
child!

(p. 514)

Echoing Walpole's partial justification for *The Castle of Otranto*,
the oldest Gothic plot of all is re-enacted in the story of the consequences of secret paternal crime. The self-consciousness and the
duplicity of the Gothic is presented in the text's doubles: Anne and
Laura, mirror images of female oppression, fortitude, passivity
and sacrifice, within and in the name of the family, are not the
only Gothic pairing. The role of villain is also doubled. One is
Sir Percival Glyde, who persecutes Anne to keep his own dark
family secret and marries Laura in the hope of dispossessing her of
her inheritance. He is the selfish, brutish example of economic and
oppressive villainy. The other, Count Fosco, is a figure of aesthetic
and imaginative villainy. His diabolical cunning and creative
intelligence are combined with a vain, self-indulgent and cruel
character that, in a corpulent body, signal him to be the real
and ambivalent object of horror. He devises the most callous
schemes with the same delight that he exhibits playing games. His
intellectual vanity and aesthetic self-consciousness are displayed
with a flourish when, in the confession he is forced to write at the
end, he recommends his idea of abducting and substituting Laura
for Anne as a model plot for English romance writers (p. 568).

As in the Radcliffean romance, the mysteries surrounding the
spectral appearance of Anne Catherick are finally furnished with
a rational explanation. Through the investigative efforts of
Walter Hartright and Marian Halcombe, Laura's relation, the
aura of mystery and terror is disclosed as an intricate but material
plot. Unlike earlier Gothic narratives, the interwoven narratives

composing the novel – lawyers' reports, domestics' statements and villain's confession – are presented as extended legal documents. The legalistic form is central to re-establishing a proper narrative against the webs of deceit woven by the villains. Law, reason and identity are thus linked as narrative forms. The careful comparison of narrative clues and temporal consistency regarding events, in the analysis of dates, times and timetables, provides the means to rescue the abducted Laura. The secret of Glyde's illegitimacy is found in a text. Moreover, it is the manipulation of stories that enables the substitution of Laura for Anne, while a properly legal account of events proves her identity and establishes her rights to her inheritance and property.

A rational explanation of criminal mysteries by means of detection and law rather than the hand of Providence situates Gothic patterns in a thoroughly Victorian context. It is an amateur detective who comes to the rescue of a persecuted wife. Female persecution and imprisonment are of a more modern cast with the asylum replacing the convent and the country house the castle. The dark labyrinth of terror is located in the city, a 'house-forest' populated by spies and conspirators (p. 379). Fosco, an adept chemist, especially when it comes to drugs, embodies the villainous potential of scientific intelligence. As a refugee from a Europe that, in 1848, was wracked by revolutionary upheavals and subversive conspiracies, he is also associated with dangerous, and imported, political ideas. The superiority of English values of law, liberty and domesticity is reaffirmed only after the terrors of losing one's identity, freedom and life have been encountered. Happy domesticity is restored in the marriage of Hartright and Laura, but only at the price of the sacrifice of her double. It is, moreover, a displaced sense of closure since, at the beginning of the novel, it was the spectral, mysterious and helpless appearance of Anne that excited Hartright's interest and became his object of desire. Sacrificed, she became a sacred and impossible object, her ghostly distance and her death a sign of the fragility of a social order caught between the duplicitous power or impotence of fathers and husbands.

Closure is partial, a sense of loss remains. Threats to law, domestic relations and cultural and sexual identity are only temporarily rebuffed. In Victorian culture, too, a loss, increasingly irreparable by reason or law alone and articulated in terms of spiritualism and horror, governs perceptions of science, nature, crime, and social degeneration. Later in the century the threats to cultural identity reappear, to be presented, in a different combination of scientific rationality and sacred horror, as distinctly sexual in nature.

7

GOTHIC RETURNS IN THE 1890s

Human beings whose nature was still natural, barbarians in
every terrible sense of the word, men of prey who were still in
possession of unbroken strength of will and lust for power, hurled
themselves on weaker, more civilized, more peaceful races,
perhaps traders or cattle raisers, or upon mellow old cultures
whose last vitality was even then flaring up in splendid fireworks
of spirit and corruption. In the beginning the noble caste was
always the barbarian caste: their predominance did not lie mainly in
physical strength but in strength of the soul – they were *more*
whole human beings (which also means, at every level, 'more
whole beasts').

(Friedrich Nietzsche, *Beyond Good and Evil*, pp. 391–2)

At the end of the nineteenth century familiar Gothic figures – the
double and the vampire – re-emerged in new shapes, with a
different intensity and anxious investment as objects of terror and
horror. Recurrent since the late eighteenth century, doubles
and vampires made an impressive reappearance in the two major
Gothic texts produced in the period, *The Strange Case of Dr Jekyll*

and Mr Hyde (1886) and *Dracula* (1897). Though harking back to Romanticism, it was in the context of Victorian science, society and culture that their fictional power was possible, associated with anxieties about the stability of the social and domestic order and the effects of economic and scientific rationality. Earlier nineteenth-century concerns about degeneration were intensified, not in relation to cities and families, but in the different threats that emerged from them, threats that were criminal and distinctly sexual in form. In scientific analyses the origin of these threats was identified in human nature itself, an internalisation that had disturbing implications for ideas about culture, civilisation and identity, as well as a socially useful potential in the process of identifying and excluding deviant and degenerate individuals. The ambivalence towards scientific issues led, in the fiction of the period, to strange realignments of the relationship between science and religion, a relationship shaped by spiritualism and the continuing popularity of the ghost story.

The ghostly returns of the past in the 1890s are both fearful and exciting incursions of barbarity and, more significantly, the irruptions of primitive and archaic forces deeply rooted in the human mind. Supernatural occurrences, also, are more than manifestations of a metaphysical power: they are associated, in scientific and quasi-religious terms, with the forces and energies of a mysterious natural dimension beyond the crude limits of rationality and empiricism, exceeding the reductive and deterministic gaze of materialistic science. These forces, seen as both unhuman and inhuman, are also in-human, embedded in the natural world and the human mind. While these powers were threatening, they were also spiritually elevating in their provision of a framework to articulate disaffections with the reductive and normalising limits of bourgeois morality and modes of production, limits whose repressions produced the divided lifestyles of the middle classes, respectable by day and pleasure-seeking by night. Individual moral degeneration was also considered as a problem of class and social structure in that capitalist modes of organisation produced a society in which individuals were parasitic upon each other. In *Civilisation* (1889), Edward Carpenter argued that primitive cultures were stronger and healthier because their members were not separated along class lines or restricted to single occupations and thus, more self-reliant, did not need to prey upon each other. In the city and the factory, where divisions of class and labour were most extreme, alienation and cultural corruption were most acute. It is no wonder that Dracula selects London as his new hunting ground.

The ambivalence of scientific theories, manifested in the indifference of Jekyll's drug to moral values, had to be contained by the cultural and moral values it threatened. Darwin's theories, by bringing humanity closer to the animal kingdom, undermined the superiority and privilege humankind had bestowed on itself. Along similar lines, the work of criminologists like Cesare Lombroso and Max Nordau attempted to discriminate between humans: some were more primitive and bestial in their nature than others. Anatomical, physiological and psychological theories were brought to bear on identifications of criminal types, those genetically determined to be degenerate and deviant. Atavism and recidivism, the regression to archaic or primitive characteristics, dominated constructions of deviance and abnormality. Physiognomy, too, was important in the process of making atavistic tendencies visible. The fiction of the period is dominated by marked descriptions of facial features as telling signs of character. In studies of the brain, theories of dual or split human nature were given a physiological basis: Paul Broca's work on the division of the brain into left and right hemispheres, one governing intellectual faculties and the other emotions, grounded dichotomies in human nature.

In disclosing threatening natural forces scientific theories gave shape to the anxieties about cultural degeneration and provided ways of disciplining and containing deviance. Combining science with religion, however, provided a new way of envisaging a sacred or metaphysical sphere. Spiritualism was one meeting place, with groups like the Society for Psychical Research, founded in 1882, legitimating investigations into paranormal powers. Science, as in *Frankenstein*'s distinction between the reductive perspective of Krempe and the visionary outlook of Waldman, disclosed new natural miracles and powers. From theories of magnetic, chemical and electrical forces the divination of greater powers was imaginable: from experiments in hypnotism, mesmerism and theories of unconscious cerebration, as Van Helsing suggests in *Dracula*, the telepathic transference of thoughts becomes a distinct possibility.

While science disclosed grand unifying powers, horror was another mode of cultural reunification, a response to the sexual figures that threatened society. One of the main objects of anxiety was the 'New Woman' who, in her demand for economic, sexual and political independence, was seen as a threat to conventionally sexualised divisions between domestic and social roles. In the loosening of moral, aesthetic and sexual codes associated with *fin de siècle* decadence, the spectre of homosexuality, as narcissistic, sensually indulgent and unnaturally perverse, constituted a form of deviance that signalled the irruption of regressive patterns of behaviour. A more pervasive, biological manifestation of the sexual threat was perceived in the form of venereal disease: syphilis was estimated to have reached epidemic proportions in the 1890s. Though linked to the immorality of certain identifiable groups and deviant behaviour, the threat of venereal disease was particularly intense as a result of its capacity to cross the boundaries that separated the healthy and respectable domestic life of the Victorian middle classes from the nocturnal worlds of moral corruption and sexual depravity.

SCIENCE, CRIME AND DESIRE

In *Jekyll and Hyde* the austere, rational and respectable world of the lawyer, Mr Utterson, is gradually eclipsed by a dark and obscure arena of mystery, violence and vice. The stark division of good and evil, in part an effect of Stevenson's Calvinism, echoes the disturbing dualities of Hogg's *Memoirs* in their uncanny relation of everyday realities and fantastic irruptions of hidden wishes. The horror emanates from the revelation of the extent and power of these buried energies. Strangely natural, the emergence of Hyde as a figure of evil is only partially explained in Gothic terms as the return of Jekyll's dark past: the 'ghost of some old sin', 'black secrets', haunt Jekyll as some suspected transgression. Jekyll's scientific practice is also implicated: his are 'transcendental' ideas, opposed to the prevailing 'narrow and material views' of his one-time colleague, Dr Lanyon (p. 80). Like Frankenstein, these visionary and metaphysical ideas have monstrous results: Enfield's first encounter with Hyde, for instance, describes him as a 'Juggernaut' callously trampling over a young girl and speculates on his preying upon the sleeping rich, drawing back their bed curtains and forcing them to succumb to his awful power (p. 37).

The story's setting suggests a Gothic image of the city in a 'dingy neighbourhood' of which Jekyll's windowless laboratory is a ruined reminder of Gothic decay, a 'sinister block' bearing 'marks of prolonged and sordid negligence'. Its 'blind forehead of discoloured wall' personifies the building with the physiognomic signs of a regressive nature. The city also recalls a primitive past: a forest, its darkness, only intensified by the glow of streetlamps, resounds with a 'low growl' (p. 38). The narrative, unlike realism's omniscient and singular perspectives, is composed of fragments, partial accounts that are gradually articulated in the disclosure of the mystery surrounding Dr Jekyll. Unlike the Gothic romance's collage of manuscripts and stories, the journals, letters and first-person narratives in *Jekyll and Hyde* are combined with legal documents, distinguishing a world dominated by professional men – lawyers, doctors and scientists. Indeed, the 'strange case' that is related is a matter of legal, medical and criminal investigation, a challenge to the mechanisms of reason, law and order. Jekyll's experiments, while possessing a diabolical, Faustian or alchemical suggestiveness, are performed with scientific instruments and chemical compounds; their results, moreover, are described in contemporary secular and scientific terms: Hyde is 'troglodytic', 'ape-like', a manifestation of human regression to primitive and animal states (pp. 40–2). Good and evil are similarly articulated as the line separating culture, progress and civilisation from barbarity, primitivism and regression. The line, however, is easily crossed: the elaborate performance that culminates in the empirical demonstration of the reversibility of human identity for Dr Lanyon makes manifest the inextricable relation of antitheses (p. 80).

Scientific theories disclose the instability of the dualities that frame cultural identity. The proximity and reversibility of good and evil cannot be restricted to a case of individual pathology: having 'no discriminating action', 'neither diabolical nor divine', the ambivalence, the moral indifference, of Jekyll's drug undermines classifications that separate normal individuals from deviant ones. Its ambivalence discloses a doubled human condition that is not symmetrical: 'although I had now two characters as well as two appearances, one was wholly evil, and the other was the same old Henry Jekyll, that incongruous compound of whose reformation and improvement I had already learned to despair' (p. 85). The drug distils evil while leaving the same old human compound of good and evil. It is no longer a question simply of good and evil, of human nature divided between a higher or better self and a lower or instinctual self, but of an ambivalence that is more disturbing to the constitution and classification of human nature. The indifference of the drug is linked to a realm of chance – accidents and circumstances beyond rational understanding or control: the success of Jekyll's experiment is due not to technical expertise, but, it is deduced, to an impurity in a particular batch of chemicals (p. 96).

The ambivalent and disturbing effects of a realm beyond human control or understanding disclose an imbalance in notions of identity that draws the 'better side' inexorably towards evil. In the guise of Hyde, Jekyll enjoys 'vicarious depravity', selfishly 'drinking pleasure with bestial avidity' (p. 86). For Hyde, Jekyll is no more than a respectable mask, a cavern in which a bandit hides from pursuit (p. 89). The unevenness of the splitting displays an inherent instability in notions of human identity. The drug, manufactured and not natural, controls and shatters 'the fortress of identity', 'rattling the doors of the prison-house of my disposition' (pp. 83–5). It is the better self, Jekyll suggests, that is both castle and prison, an external image that is shaken by the drug taken internally. Identity, moreover, seems to be an effect of images, shaping and crossing the boundaries of inside and outside. Seeing the 'ugly idol in the glass' does not, as the phrase implies, evoke revulsion on the part of Jekyll. It is a welcome image, as natural and human as any other: 'this, too, was myself. It seemed natural and human'. The image of Hyde, moreover, is also more unifed, seeming 'more express and single, than the imperfect and divided countenance, I had hitherto been accustomed to call mine' (pp. 4–5). While the repetition of 'seem' implies a distinction between deceptive appearance and true reality, conventions associated with images of personal identity are, in the rather disinterested tones of the word 'accustomed', presented as strangely arbitrary. At this point, also, the conventional dualities invoked by Jekyll in terms of a difference between his 'original and better self' (p. 89) and a lower or secondary self are undermined. The secondary self seems primary, growing in power in inverse proportion to the sickliness of the better self. The doubling in the novel, then, does not establish or fix the boundaries of good and evil, self and other, but discloses the ambivalence of identity and the instability of the social, moral and scientific codes that manufacture distinctions. These external structures are seen to be crucial as well as disturbing and contradictory. Hyde uses Jekyll to escape reprimand and punishment, while the latter preserves his respectable reputation and enjoys vicarious pleasures in the guise of the former. Jekyll owes his existence to the law since, without it, he would be of no use to Hyde. These external pressures sustain his better self: 'I think I was glad to have my better impulses thus buttressed and guarded by the terrors of the scaffold' (p. 91). His hesitancy regarding the external legal supports for his inner being is elaborated in the ambivalence the story uncovers in the law itself. While the law buttresses the fortress of identity called Jekyll, it also produces the radical evil called Hyde, and the ambivalent doubling they both employ as a masquerade against punishment. Law, establishing particular limits between good and evil as taboos and prohibitions, also produces the desires that can only be manifested secretly, in the guise of an other being.

The production of illegitimate desires, and their construction as unnatural by a system that is itself seen to be arbitrary, has a significant bearing on the cultural context of the novel. The supposedly natural power of law, presented in Jekyll's paternal interest in Hyde (p. 89), is strangely unbalanced: the exclusively male world of the novel itself seems unnatural, an unnaturalness reflected in the speculations concerning the relationship between Jekyll and Hyde: the mirror in Jekyll's cabinet is offered as evidence of a horrible kind of narcissism. In Oscar Wilde's *The Picture of Dorian Gray* (1891) the portrait as an inverted image is, like the mirror, bound up with the reversibility of individualised good and evil as well as homosexuality. Moreover, the idea that Hyde is blackmailing Jekyll, and the luxurious, indulgent but tasteful decoration of Hyde's rooms imply a past relation of some intimacy and the unnaturalness of homosexual pleasures. The associations of unnaturalness with homosexuality, however, seem to be undercut rather than reinforced in a text in which notions of human nature are neither stable nor dual, but bound up with an ambivalence and uncertainty that leaves boundaries between nature, culture, law and identity both in doubt and strangely interconnected.

While the doubling of *Jekyll and Hyde* discloses horrors and questions concerning human nature and sexuality in terms of law and science, other versions of atavism employ different fictional and discursive arrangements, involving mythological figures from the past and the occult and contemporary scientific practice. In Arthur Machen's *The Great God Pan* (1894) a scientist specialising in cerebral physiology and also, like Jekyll, a doctor of 'transcendental medicine', rearranges a few cells in the brain of a woman patient and produces startling and occult results: she encounters 'the great god Pan', becomes a gibbering wreck and dies nine months later after giving birth to a daughter. The narrative gradually pieces together the ghastly incidents that surround the daughter's life, though she takes on many disguises. Her power seems to be of a terrifyingly sexual nature, seducing her male victims, often from the respectable echelons of society, before revealing to them something so unspeakably horrible that they commit suicide. As a daughter of Pan, the woman reveals secret forces at the heart of things, forces that should, the narrator moralises, remain buried, no doubt because their sexual nature is linked to female desire. The mythological and occult frame, moreover, presents science as a kind of alchemy, dabbling with powerful forces it cannot understand and producing effects it cannot control. In 'The Novel of the White Powder', from *The Three Imposters* (1895), science opens on to a similarly occult dimension. A serious law student, after taking a drug prescribed by his doctor, becomes a decadent pleasure-seeker before regressing totally into a horrible mass of black primordial slime. Theories of atavism are rendered occult: scientific analysis explains that the drug obtained from a perfectly respectable chemist's shop had been affected by a long process of temperature variations that turned it into the *vinum sabbati*, the potion for a witches' sabbath. More than simply reformulating regression in terms of the occult, the conclusion places science within a greater, sacred and mystical universe of force and energy, matter and spirit.

VAMPIRES

The play between mythological and modern significance, between mystical and scientific visions of horror and unity, sexuality and sacred violence, is focused in the figure of the vampire. In Mary Braddon's 'Good Lady Ducayne' (1896) the vampire theme signals the barbarities that result from human vanity and scientific illusions. Centring on a naïve young companion growing weaker and weaker from a mysterious 'mosquito bite', the mystery is explained as a series of blood transfusions designed to extend her old and withered mistress's life beyond natural limits. A scientific version of the quest for eternal life, the story highlights the horrible illusions of alchemical powers that surround contemporary science. In contrast, Sheridan Le Fanu's 'Carmilla' (1874) makes no attempt to rationalise superstition within the bounds of everyday realism or nineteenth-century science. The Gothic features of the narrative temporally and geographically distance the story from the present. The events are framed as a case from the files of Le Fanu's psychic doctor, Martin Hesslius. Castles, ruins, chapels and tombs signal the Gothic tradition and its atmosphere of mystery and superstition. At the centre of the mystery is 'Carmilla', a beautiful young woman who arrives at the castle of an aristocratic family. Uncannily, Carmilla is the very image of a figure who appeared, years before, in a childhood dream of the family's daughter Laura. The latter, attracted to and repulsed by Carmilla, establishes an intimate acquaintance. Deaths occur in the locality, accompanied by superstitious rumblings. Oblivious, Laura soon becomes the prey of Carmilla. Laura is saved however, by the intervention of the guardian of one of Carmilla's other victims. As vampire lore is expounded, and her tomb discovered, Carmilla is subjected to the traditional measures of decapitation and a stake through the heart, a perfectly natural end in a story in which superstition, legend and folklore are part of the everyday reality.

The story's sexual images, none the less, have a resonance in the context of the late nineteenth century. Female sexuality, embodied in Carmilla's languor and fluidity, is linked, in her ability to turn into a large black cat, with witchcraft and contemporary visions of sexual, primitive regression and independent femininity: feline, darkly sensual and threatening in its underlying, cruel violence, Carmilla's unnatural desires are signalled in her choice of females as her victims and the alluring as well as disturbing effects she has on them. Exciting amorous emotions in Laura that are far from innocent, the attraction is shadowed by an incomprehensible fear and anxiety when Carmilla's romantic passions are articulated in terms of blood, sacrifice and fatal possession. Laura's susceptibility to Carmilla's disturbing charms is finally interrupted by the reassertion of a male order of meaning and sexual differentiation. The secrets of Carmilla's behaviour and her resemblance to an old portrait are explained as vampiric immortality. Her changing yet singular identity is disclosed as a play on words: she has masqueraded under names that are anagrams of Carmilla. The curiously ambivalent power, the superstitious allure of the vampire herself, lingers in the memory of Laura, haunted by the dual images of 'beautiful girl' and 'writing fiend' (p. 314), images that only partially described the polymorphous representations of female sexuality.

As a haunting figure from past narratives like legends and folklore, and as an irruption of unavowable energies from the primitive past of human sexuality, the vampire remains disturbingly ambivalent. The female vampires in *Dracula* display the effects of desire and horror attendant on the dangerous doubleness of sexuality. In Stoker's use of the legend, however, the principal vampire is male, a feature in line with the legacy of Gothic villainy and Dr Polidori's Romantic and Byronic hero, Lord Ruthven, in 'The Vampyre' (1818). Wresting diabolical ambivalence and agency from its association, in 'Carmilla' and a whole host of other tales of female demon lovers, Stoker's novel subordinates feminine sexuality to a masculine perspective in which women serve as objects of exchange and competition between men. *Dracula* recuperates the Gothic romance in making men the primary subjects of terror and horror, thereby addressing and attempting to redress, in its movement between figures of the past and present, the uncanny mobility of normal, natural and sexual boundaries in the 1890s. Akin to Radcliffe's Montoni, Polidori's Ruthven and Maturin's Melmoth, the malevolence of the Count, his pale, gaunt features, demonic eyes and callous libertinism are bolstered by supernatural attributes of metamorphosis, flight and immortality. Dracula's heritage extends deeper into the Gothic past: the account of his family history is full of tribal migrations and conquests, a militaristic, warrior past characterised by values of blood and honour (pp. 42–3). This history is, in part, that of the romance as traced by eighteenth-century antiquarians: stories of uncertain origin, romances, according to different versions, began among the nomadic warlike tribes of northern Europe or peoples migrating from the East. The Carpathians formed the crossroads where these traditions met. The vampire is not only associated with the dissemination of the romance. In travellers' accounts from the eighteenth century onwards the significance of the vampire in the folklore, superstitions and customs of Eastern peoples was recorded and assessed. The origins of the vampire were explained as fears of the Plague, thought, since the Middle Ages, to have emanated from the East. Dracula's principal companions and alternative forms – rats, wolves and bats – were associated with disease.

In the setting of *Dracula* stock features of the Gothic novel make a magnificent reappearance: the castle is mysterious and forbidding, its secret terrors and splendid isolation in a wild and mountainous region form as sublime a prison as any building in which a Gothic heroine was incarcerated. The place of a heroine, however, is taken by the naïve young lawyer Harker. Throughout the novel ruins, graveyards and vaults – all the macabre and gloomy objects of morbid fascination and melancholy – signal the awful presence of the Gothic past. Dracula is more than a Gothic villain, however, more than the mercenary and mundane bandit that they too often turn out to be. As the sublime synthesis of the human and supernatural terrors of Gothic writing, he is both villain and ghostly diabolical agent whose magic and power cannot be reduced to mere tricks or effects of overindulgent, superstitious imagination: more than rational, he serves to elicit rather than dispel superstitious beliefs, demanding, not a return to reason and morality, but a reawakening of spiritual energies and sacred awe. The form of the novel testifies to the excessive, unpresentable nature of this demand. The letters and journal entries telling different but connected parts of the same story compose a whole whose immensity, like the unrepresentable horror of Dracula's unreflecting image, remains obscure.

Dracula's narrative fragments are of a distinctly modern cast. Though alluding to the Gothic devices of lost manuscripts and letters, *Dracula*'s fragments are recorded in the most modern manner: by typewriter, in shorthand and on phonograph. There are other indicators of modern systems of communication: telegrams, newspaper cuttings, train timetables are all signs of contemporaneity as are the medical and psychiatric classifications, the legal documents and the letters of commercial transaction. Not only useful in recording the story, these systems provide the information necessary to follow Dracula's trail and investigate his plot. The modernity of the novel's setting is also signalled by the professional status of the men who combine against the vampire: apart from the aristocratic leftover, Arthur Holmwood, they are lawyers and doctors at the centre of late Victorian commercial life. Even Mina, by no means a 'New Woman', acknowledges in her secretarial abilities shifts in the nature of work within and outside the family. Van Helsing is a combination of professor, doctor, lawyer, philosopher and scientist. Like his former student, Dr Seward, and his systems for classifying psychiatric disorders in his asylum, Van Helsing is well versed in contemporary theories: the criminology of Lombroso and Nordau is cited, as are the ideas of Charcot concerning hypnotism and the notion of unconscious cerebration. Dracula's archaic, primal energy is reformulated in scientific terms: his 'child-brain' a sign of criminal regression which is also characterised by his egocentricity (p. 389). Renfield, the inmate of Seward's asylum and 'index' of the Count's proximity, also displays the characteristic criminal traits of secrecy and selfishness. In his strange eating habits, progressing from flies to spiders, sparrows and, he hopes, kittens, Renfield selects a bizarre food chain which links animal to human life in a caricature of Darwinian theory. Reconstructing natural events with its scientific explanations, modernity also supplants the myths, the explanations of the past, with its own version of things: the occult powers of Dracula's castle, Van Helsing suggests, might well be natural, mysterious forces of geological and chemical origin (p. 411).

Modernity's progress, threatened by Dracula throughout the novel, is not as secure as its explanations suggest. As Harker observes: 'unless my senses deceive me, the old centuries had, and have, powers of their own which mere modernity cannot kill' (p. 51). Irrepressible forces from the past continue to threaten the present's idea of itself. In response to the deficiencies of contemporary culture and society, in part embodied in its scientific values, the science in *Dracula* does not simply replace superstition with deterministic knowledge, the latter bound up with cultural degeneration and the parasitic nature of capitalist social organisation. A want of culturally unifying and elevating values underlies the repeated invocation of sacred forms in the novel. The threat of wanton and corrupt sexuality is horrifically displayed in vampiric shape. Their decadence, nocturnal existence and indiscriminate desires distinguish vampires as a particularly modern sexual threat to cultural mores and taboos: they are modern visions of epidemic contagions from the past, visited on the present in a form that, like venereal disease, enters the home only after (sexual) invitation.

Against the threats of contagion and disintegration a sacred order is reconstituted. Dispensing with its inadequate materialism, science offers grander visions of a mysterious and sacred universe. Van Helsing is more than a scientist: he is also a metaphysician who deals with 'spiritual pathology' as well as physical disease, a psychic investigator or transcendental doctor like Le Fanu's Hesselius or Stevenson's Jekyll. Van Helsing does not discount superstition and is the first to use sacred objects like the crucifix and the Host. Science involves mysteries and opens on to a more than rational plane in line with Victorian attitudes towards spiritualism and psychic investigation. The fusion of scientific knowledge and religious values is made possible by the demonic threat of Dracula: his diabolical powers and primitive energy, leading to a 'baptism of blood' for his victims (p. 414), mark the utter profanity that demands a more than rational response.

Under the unifying and priestly command of Van Helsing the men of middle-class Victorian England reinvigorate their cultural identity and primal masculinity in the sacred values that are reinvoked against the sublimity of the vampiric threat. In the face of the voluptuous and violent sexuality loosed by the decadently licentious vampire, a vigorous sense of patriarchal, bourgeois and family values is restored. Out of the collective fragments of the text a new masculine image is assembled in opposition to the dark, inverted figure of pure evil and negativity. Dracula is the dark double of the brave and unselfish men whose identity is forged in their struggle; he is the regressive in-human otherness lifted from the realm of individual psychopathology into a cultural field as its absolute antithesis. Without mirror image or shadow, Dracula is a pure inversion. On a symbolic level he is the mirror and shadow of Victorian masculinity, a monstrous figure of male desire that distinguishes what men are becoming from what they should become. He forms a mirror that must be destroyed since its already fragmented textual composition signals regressive narcissism, perverse egoism and a terrible duplicity of appearance, unreality and un/naturalness that threatens all cultural values and distinctions. Dracula's duplicity is multiple, doubling Harker by donning his clothes in order that his disappearance is not linked to the castle. Dracula is also a foreigner trying to pass as English. On a symbolic level he passes for Christ, Beast and various identities within the family. This has the effect, as in the case of his interception of Harker's true letters and ordering him to write brief notes, of a dissimulative disruption of proper systems of communication.

Dracula's crossing of boundaries is relentless: returning from the past he tyrannises the present, uncannily straddling the borders between life and death and thereby undoing a fundamental human fact. In crossing the borders between East and West he undoes cultural distinctions between civilisation and barbarity, reason and irrationality, home and abroad. Dracula's threat is his poly-morphousness, both literally, in the shapes he assumes, and symbolically in terms of the distinctions he upsets. His significance is dangerously overdetermined: in the scene where he is interrupted in the act of pressing Mina's mouth to his bleeding breast he appears as an inversion of Christ as Pelican, nourishing his subjects with his blood in an unholy communion, and as a mother suckling Mina with the milk of his blood. 'The blood is the life', as Renfield reiterates throughout the novel. The exchange of bodily fluids renders the scene shockingly sexual, its violence as masculine as any act of rape. Blood, indeed, is linked to semen: Arthur, after giving blood to his fiancé, Lucy, states that he feels as if they are married. The fluid exchanges present a perverse sexuality, unnatural in the way it exceeds fixed gender roles and heterosexual distinctions. Dracula's fluid, shifting and amorphous shape is, like Carmilla's, threatening because it has no singular or stable nature or identity. Meanings, identities and proper family boundaries are utterly transgressed in the movements of vampiric desire and energy. For all his sovereignty and violence, Dracula is, in respect of his polymorphousness, strangely feminised and, like Lucy, condensed into an objectification of total excess, 'a Thing' (p. 277, p. 293), as inhuman, 'hellish' and 'inorganic' as Hyde (*Jekyll and Hyde*, pp. 94–5). Lucy is presented as a 'Thing' just before the band of men symbolically subject her to phallic law by driving a stake through her heart and decapitating her. Restoring the boundaries between life and death, body and soul, earth and heaven, the ritualised killing of vampires reconstitutes properly patriarchal order and fixes cultural and symbolic meanings. The vampire is constructed as absolute object, the complete antithesis of subjectivity, agency and authority. The ritual killing also restores systems of communication in which women remain objects for male exchange. By way of women Dracula attacks men; through women he will contaminate and colonise the teeming metropolis of London. In the name of women the good men respond to the threat. Through and over women their bonds, relations and identities are established, Lucy, for instance, being courted by Arthur, Quincey and Seward.

Women constitute the objects and supports for male exchanges and identities, supports that are narcissistic in their reflections on and between men. Dracula's mirror thus returns the novel to its specific cultural and sexual context even as it serves to project sacred identities into a universal, metaphysical dimension. Dracula's effects, imaginarily, in the way individuals perceive his threat, and symbolically, in the cultural significance assigned to him, are infectious, producing doubles and reversals in images that contaminate all limits. As the males of the novel consolidate themselves against Dracula they begin to duplicate as well as reverse his effects. The mirror that Dracula composes for them becomes a mirror of male desire, of what men, in the 1890s, have to become in order to survive. The hunter becomes the hunted, and vice versa, as Dracula is driven out of western Europe. In the process western civilisation and rationality grow increasingly barbaric and irrational. Superstition, both religious and folkloric, takes precedence over reason. Male emotions become more visible:

Van Helsing lapses into hysteria after Lucy's funeral (p. 225); Arthur sobs hysterically on the paternal and maternal shoulder of the professor after impaling her and later bursts into tears in Mina's arms (p. 279, p. 295). Having found its maternal place by arriving on Mina's shoulder, male hysteria is a sign of the breakdown and longing for proper social bonds. These are nostalgically invoked by Quincey in his recalling of 'yarns by the campfire', dressing 'one another's wounds' and drinking 'healths on the shore of Titacaca' (p. 83). The bonding produced by exclusively male adventures forms an idyllic boy-scout past that is reconstituted and sanctified in the pursuit of the vampire. In the final stages of the chase Seward observes how 'those adventurous days of ours are turning up useful' (p. 461). Van Helsing appeals to this spirit when he describes how the vampire may be beaten by the 'power of combination' and the unselfish devotion to a cause (p. 306). It is a cause that requires the letting of blood. In an earlier context, Van Helsing says to Quincey 'a brave man's blood is the best thing on this earth when a woman is in trouble. You're a man, and no mistake. Well, the devil may work against us for all he's worth, but God sends us men when we want them' (p. 194). The jolly fortitude of this statement is tested later when Quincey loses more than the amount of blood required in a transfusion.

Manhood, blood and bravery form the cornerstones of Van Helsing's fatherly notion of cultural and spiritual renewal. The appeal to male strength, blood and bravery culminates in the violence of the hunt that marks the return of a buried warrior tradition represented and mourned at the beginning of the novel by Dracula's description of his heritage: 'the warlike days are over. Blood is too precious a thing in these days of dishonourable peace; and the glories of the great races are as a tale that is told' (p. 43). Engaging in battle with Dracula, Van Helsing's vampire-killers reawaken racial memories and myths of blood and honour: Quincey is described as a 'moral viking' and Arthur is compared to Thor as he impales Lucy (p. 225, p. 277). To combat the racial myths associated with the creature originating in the East, myths of northern tribes, myths linked to Gothic notions of freedom and strength, are invoked. A warlike paganism is combined with Christianity, a sacralisation of racial myths whose function within an embattled and aggressive cultural and imperialist imagination is starkly emphasised when Van Helsing invokes divine sanction for their project: in God's name they 'go out as the old knights of the Cross' (p. 412). The appeal to past history and romance is not merely invocative of a fictional tradition: it alludes to the belligerent pursuit of a religious cause, in the Crusades, against the non-Christian peoples of the East. In the context of Gothic fiction this seems like a nostalgic appeal to a long-dead world, a dis-appeared past imagined as noble, strong and purposeful. It is also a return to myths and fictions that reinvent a sacred unity for the degenerate 1890s. The return to myth, the invocation of romantic fictions within a Gothic fiction, has an uncanny effect on the values of domesticity and patriarchy whose superiority, stability and naturalness are finally affirmed at the close of the novel. These start to seem like myths themselves. Indeed, throughout the novel there are no examples of model families. The only biological parents, Lucy's mother and Arthur's father, die, while other paternal and maternal figures are only surrogates: Hawkins bequeathes his property to Harker and Mina in a fatherly gesture, Van Helsing is a good father to everyone, as Mina is their mother. Dracula is allotted the role of bad father. The absence of family underlines the nostalgia for the family that is literalised by the birth of a child at the end. Structurally inscribed throughout the novel in the paternal and maternal duplicates, the myth is only realised in the closure of the fiction.

The making real of this mythical model of the family demands, for a culture disintegrating without it, blood, expulsion and sacrifice: family values are restored by the ritual destruction of Dracula and the sacrifice of female sexuality embodied by Lucy, and are vitally monumentalised in the self-sacrificing death of

Quincey and his subsequent and nominal immortalisation in the Christian name of the Harkers' son. The romance quest provides the structure of a male fantasy of sacred, immortal power, of its originary values restored in the present by violent, sacrificial energy. The horror embodied by Dracula reawakens the primitive and powerful emotions of his opponents, emotions of attraction and repulsion in which his intimate doubleness is expelled and repeated in another terrible expenditure of energy. Civilisation and domesticity needs to retain and channel its buried natural, even barbaric energies, signified in hunter and warrior myths: its spirit, unity, strength and immortality are nourished by the undead myths of its own duplicitous self-image.

Turning the Gothic romance into a male quest romance, *Dracula* feeds off prevailing cultural anxieties concerning corruption, sexuality and spirit. For Van Helsing, the penetration of evil mysteries and the redemption of proper identities by means of sacred horror involve clerical and ideological powers. As a scientist and psychic doctor his powers are rational and more than rational like the world investigated by Hesselius and another popular, secular and yet strangely magical figure, the detective, as exemplified by Arthur Conan Doyle's Sherlock Holmes. The mysteries, terrors and horrors explained by his penetrating mind, endowed with a rationality that seems more than rational, are, though ultimately mundane and deviously criminal, imbued with an aura of the fantastic, spectral and diabolical. *Dracula*'s adventurous romance also alludes to the tales of adventure that, from Scott's romances onwards, provide a more popular and exciting alternative to domestic realism. The associations of Dracula with the East are important in this respect. For the East, at the high point of Victorian imperialism, provided many wonderful adventures and strange tales, which, in Kipling's stories about India and, similarly, in Rider Haggard's narratives of Africa, projected the darkness of Gothic fears and desires on to other cultures, peoples and places.

8

TWENTIETH-CENTURY GOTHIC

The nineteenth and twentieth centuries have given us as much
terror as we can take. We have paid a high enough price for the
nostalgia of the whole and the one, for the reconciliation of
the concept and the sensible, of the transparent and the
communicable experience. Under the general demand for
slackening and for appeasement, we can hear the mutterings
of the desire for a return of terror, for the realization of the fantasy
to seize reality.

(Jean-Francois Lyotard, *The Postmodern Condition*, pp. 81–2)

The necessity of always focusing somewhere else, of never seeking
the other in the terrifying illusion of dialogue but instead following
the other like the other's own shadow, and circumscribing him.
Never being oneself – but never being alienated either: coming
from without to inscribe oneself on the figure of the Other,
within that strange form from elsewhere, that secret form
which orders not only chains of events but also existences in their
singularity.

(Jean Baudrillard, *The Transparency of Evil*, p. 174)

In the twentieth century Gothic is everywhere and nowhere.
Michael Jackson's video for the song 'Thriller' runs the gamut of

visual mutations of terror which, though alluding to Gothic meta-morphoses, draws widely on the images popularised in cinematic representations of horror. It has been the cinema that has sustained Gothic fiction in the twentieth century by endlessly filming versions of the classic Gothic novels. In this respect, Gothic, always nour-ished in popular culture, is perfectly at home. Film versions have supplanted the more literary, written, fictions in the popular imagination to the extent that certain actors, Bela Lugosi and Boris Karloff particularly, virtually usurped the villains they played. *Bauhaus*, among the post-Punk bands associated with the inception of 'Goth' musical and sartorial styles in the late 1970s in Britain, did not celebrate Dracula in their first single, but the actor: 'Bela Lugosi is Dead' and, of course, undead as well. In other areas, the dispersion and transformation that occurred throughout the nineteenth century accelerates in the twentieth in a diffusion and proliferation of genres and media that are related, often only tenuously, to Gothic. Perhaps the strangest use of Gothic in the twentieth century is Isak Dinesen's very conventional renderings of themes in her short stories. In the continuing popularity of ghost stories, in the development of fantastic, horror and occult fiction, in canonical modernist writing, especially German and American work, Gothic shadows flicker among representations of cultural, familial and individual fragmentation, in uncanny disruptions of the boundaries between inner being, social values and concrete reality and in modern forms of barbarism and monstrosity. Science fiction, connected with the Gothic since *Frankenstein*, presents new objects of terror and horror in strangely mutated life-forms and alien invaders from other and future worlds. With science fiction, however, there is significant divergence from Gothic strategies: cultural anxieties in the present are no longer projected on to the past but are relocated in the future.

The prevalence of scientific devices and experiments as causes of tales of terror and horror is part of a shift in the objects and effects of awful emotion. Unlike previous Gothic incarnations, scientific themes are not opposed to spiritual or religious modes of understanding or organising the world. Though these discourses pervade humanism, it is ideas of human individuality and community that are sacralised in horrified reactions to science. Located in a thoroughly secular world, science signifies the oppressive domination of technological production, bureaucratic organisation and social regulation. What is lost and recovered in the confrontation with scientifically-inspired machines, mutants and inhuman, automated worlds is a virtually religious sense of human wholeness and agency.

The loss of human identity and the alienation of self from both itself and the social bearings in which a sense of reality is secured are presented in the threatening shapes of increasingly dehumanised environments, machinic doubles and violent, psychotic fragmentation. These disturbances are linked to a growing disaffection with the structures and dominant forms of modernity, forms that have become characterised as narratives themselves, powerful and pervasive myths shaping the identities, institutions and modes of production that govern everyday life. In this 'postmodern condition' the breakdown of modernity's metanarratives discloses a horror that identity, reality, truth and meaning are not only effects of narratives but subject to a dispersion and multiplication of meanings, realities and identities that obliterates the possibility of imagining any human order and unity. Progress, rationality and civilisation, increasingly suspect, cede to new forms of sublimity and excess, new terrors, irrationalities and inhumanities. In the questioning of narratives of authority and the legitimacy of social forms, what can be called postmodern Gothic is akin, in its playfulness and duplicity, to the artificialities and ambivalences that surrounded eighteenth-century Gothic writing and were produced in relation to the conflicts of emerging modernity.

MODERN GOTHIC WRITING

Much of the writing linked to Gothic in the early part of the twentieth century is carried over from later nineteenth-century styles. Objects of anxiety take their familiar forms from earlier manifestations: cities, houses, archaic and occult pasts, primitive energies, deranged individuals and scientific experimentation are the places from which awesome and inhuman terrors and horrors are loosed on an unsuspecting world. For the American writer Ambrose Bierce, haunted houses predominate as sombre sites on which the past returns to disturb the present. Evil and transgression are gently suggested in these hauntings and the atmosphere is more one of melancholy and morbid fascination. There is a similar restraint in many of M. R. James's ghost stories, set in the college and library environments and the East Anglian countryside he used to frequent. The tales have an antiquarian Gothic atmosphere in which scholars and academics discover supernatural revenants through old manuscripts and artefacts bearing runic and mysterious inscriptions. While stories like 'Count Magnus' ([1904] 1987) describe the eponymous villain's violent returns from the grave, the distanced narratives and historical and scholarly concerns leave distinctions between supernaturalism and reality relatively intact, the one only having mildly disturbing effects on the other. In 'Oh, Whistle, And I'll Come to You, My Lad' ([1904] 1987), a Professor with no time for ideas of the supernatural finds an ancient bronze whistle with mysterious inscriptions on it. He blows it, to be pursued by an invisible form. Saved from falling from a window, the Professor leaves the inn where he was staying and, with little explanation and no rationalisation the story ends perfunctorily: 'there is nothing more to tell, but, as you may imagine, the Professor's views on certain points are less clear than they used to be' (p. 77).

Understated and gently suggestive of terror in stories that detail brief incursions of one world upon another, James's use of the

Gothic also departs in the direction of the fiction of the occult. 'Casting the Runes' ([1911] 1987), set in a world of museums and scholarly publication, compiles the fragmentary story of a researcher's occult vengeance using ancient lore and runic curses. The mystical world of occult lore, popular in the nineteenth century with writers like Bulwer-Lytton and Machen, develops in two directions that, like the Gothic, either rationalise or myth-ologise occult powers. Algernon Blackwood, in 'Ancient Sorceries' (1908) does the former. A story of an English tourist's visit to a sleepy French village whose population are really witches, turning into cats on their sabbath, its events are explained by the psychic doctor, John Silence, to whom the case is related, as an effect of ancestral memory, since the tourist's family once lived in the place. In H. P. Lovecraft's work a complete, fantastic 'Chtulu' mythology is developed. In works like *The Lurker at the Threshold* (1945) ancient, powerful beings ejected from the earth that they once ruled threaten to invade and reclaim their dominion. These occult fantasies, like the fabulous dimensions of ancient and imagined worlds in J. R. R. Tolkien's fiction, seem wishful escapes from twentieth-century life. In Mervyn Peake's fantastic Gormenghast trilogy – *Titus Groan* (1946), *Gormenghast* (1950) and *Titus Alone* (1959), the Gothic forms, like the castle and its lord, and the Dickensian Gothicisation of industrial and pedagogical horrors, counterbalance fantasy with a grotesque glance at the nightmares of the twentieth century.

Gothic reflections on the structures of modernity are also evident in other literary forms. Joseph Conrad's *Heart of Darkness* (1902) questions the uncomplicated imperialism of adventure stories, like those popularised by Rider Haggard, that reinforce constructions of the savagery and otherness of Africa's 'dark continent'. In Conrad's frame narrative of a journey in pursuit of a colonial trader, Kurtz, who has become immersed in the culture and environment he was supposed to be exploiting, the encounter is less of white western civilisation with black African barbarity, less an external threat of an alien and dangerous culture, and more a horrified recognition of the darkness within late Victorian society and values. The horror, in *Heart of Darkness*, becomes political terror in *The Secret Agent* (1907), the locus of fear shifted from colonial outposts to the centre of the British Empire. The London of *The Secret Agent* is the dark and labyrinthine areas of industrial production and working-class housing, populated by anarchists and political activists, émigrés from European states engaged in terroristic conspiracies: the threat is very much within.

Some of the most disturbingly Gothic images of the twentieth century appear in the writings of Franz Kafka, writings which vacillate between subjective and objective positions, between the horrors of individual alienation and self-loathing and the grotesquely distorted images of everyday family and social life. The focus on disturbed psychological states, on social alienation and inner turmoil, relates to the horrors glimpsed by darker Romantics like Godwin, Shelley, Hogg and Poe. In 'Metamorphosis' (1916) a young man awakes to find he has become an insect. An image of self-loathing, it also serves, in the domestic context in which it is situated, as a projection of the anxieties regarding family structure and feeling. In *The Trial* (1925) individual guilt is inscribed throughout social and legal systems as a mysterious, arbitrary and impenetrable condition: the hero, Josef K, lost in a bewildering Gothic labyrinth of bureaucracy and indifferent regulations, never discovers the nature of the crime of which he is accused. The unapproachable and unfathomable nature of law and authority is presented, in *The Castle* (1926), as the looming, dark and distant edifice of Gothic terror.

The sense of a grotesque, irrational and menacing presence pervading the everyday, and causing its decomposition, emerges in the Gothic fiction produced, predominately, in the Southern states of America. Centred on houses in the tradition established by Poe, in 'The Fall of the House of Usher', the disintegration of the normal and familiar in Southern Gothic signals the decay of family and culture. The disjointed perspectives of William Faulkner's fiction present a decaying, grotesque and absurd world through the disturbed consciousness of misfits and malcontents often on the verge of insanity. In women's writing of the period the internalisation of Gothic forms of decay, fear and fragmentation reflect important sexual differences. Charlotte Perkins Gilman's 'The Yellow Wallpaper' (1892) updates Gothic themes of female oppression and imprisonment in an account of the psychological effects that a doctor's isolated 'rest cure' has on his wife. 'Clytie' (1941), by Eudora Welty, describes the oppressive atmosphere perceived by a woman in an utterly disintegrated family. The sense of despair culminates in a moment of nauseous self-recognition and a grotesque final image of suicide: ladylike stockings protruding from the house's rain-barrel like a pair of tongs. In Flannery O'Connor's fiction female sexuality, identity and fears about maternity are represented in the grotesque shapes of Gothic horror. The internal focus of Southern Gothic is manifested in the predominance of subjective states that grotesquely distort boundaries between fantasy and reality. A recent and very significant revision and extension of the American Gothic tradition is performed in Toni Morrison's *Beloved* (1987). The haunted house, and the ghostly reminder of transgression which inhabits it, provide the scene for a narrative that moves between the past and the present to uncover, in the interweaving of a repressed individual history with a suppressed cultural history, the external and internal effects of racial oppression.

In popular fictional genres, romantic, horror and science fiction especially, echoes of Gothic features abound. Daphne du Maurier's *Rebecca* (1938), for example, uses Gothic patterns in a domestic context in her story of the way a dead wife continues to haunt the living in the effects of guilt, anxiety and suspicion her memory produces. The many variations in objects and places of terror in modern horror fiction exceed Gothic in the forms and sources of violence and destruction that are used. None the less, some novels still include Gothic features. In Stephen King's *The Shining* (1977) an old, deserted and isolated hotel is the site of terror while a family are its victims. As a place of shinings, projections of violent disturbances in the past or future, the hotel acts as a magnifying glass or mirror for psychic energies and psychotic impulses of certain events and individuals, an uncanny movement in which interior tendencies and external environment exacerbate each other. Affected by the hotel, the father becomes more and more psychotic while his son glimpses the spectral returns of past scenes of violence.

SCIENCE FICTION AND FILM

In science fiction horror finds even more numerous and varied objects and sources. Its origins, however, are linked to texts like *Frankenstein*, one of the Romantic works that impressed the writer most influential in the science fictional reformulation of Gothic strategies, H. G. Wells. Anxieties pervading Victorian culture at the end of the nineteenth century are addressed in works like *The Island of Dr Moreau* (1896) with its eponymous mad scientist performing a strange variation on Darwinian theory by populating an island with his bizarre and monstrous experimental creatures, and in the threat of alien invasion in *The War of the Worlds* (1898). Moreau's creations are both unnatural and beyond human control while the alien invaders are clinically, technologically, inhumanly and callously, scientifically indifferent: unlike the vampire, who feeds lasciviously on human blood, the aliens inject it. Humanity is left in question by the nightmare vision of other and future worlds: in *Dr Moreau* pathological individuals loose uncontrollable forces and in *The War of the Worlds* the aliens are expelled, not as a result of human endeavour but because bacteria, against which they have no biological defence, contaminate their constitutions. Threatened by alien machines, humanity is also threatened by conceptions in which it is perceived as a biological mechanism among a host of other, competing mechanisms. In the identification of terror and horror as forces encroaching on the present from the future rather than the past, Wells inaugurates an important departure that renders many of the uncanny devices of Gothic fiction obsolete: while the irruption of terror from the past served as a way to evoke emotions that reconstituted human values, the future only presents a dark, unknown space from which horrors are visited.

In the fiction and film associated with cyberculture, the artificial forms that are given life and consciousness project current anxieties about disintegrating Western cultural and social formations on to a nightmarish vision of the future. The cyberpunk novel *Neuromancer* (1984), by William Gibson, is set in a future run by large corporations and controlled by computers. The homogenised corporate and silicon order is maintained in relation to the diasporic proliferation of subcultures centred on drugs, violence and terror. Humans are little more than adjuncts to machines, cast aside as economically unproductive detritus or rebuilt in accordance with technological needs and capacities, leaving nature and humanity supplemented to the point of extinction. However, the 'romance' signalled in the title is far from insignificant. For all the prosthetic implants, the 'jackings in' of individuals' neural networks into the cyberspace of computerised matrices, the novel retains a distinctly romantic plot, underlined by references to fictional precursors like vampires. The hero, a 'cyberspace cowboy' named Case, is enjoined to participate in an attempt, by an odd collection of misfits, to penetrate the defenses of the castle-like home of the family controlling the two most powerful Artificial Intelligences in the world, Neuromancer and Wintermute. This place, the Villa Straylight, is a 'Gothic folly' (p. 206). In the labyrinth of this building and, for Case, in the labyrinthine networks of cyberspace, the denouement is achieved: the two computers are enabled to synthesise, creating an absolutely new form of life.

The fusion of old and new forms of romance recurs throughout science fiction. In the modernising of earlier terrors and horrified encounters with life that virtually replicates human existence, the nature and essence associated with the human figure are rendered uncertain, if not obsolete. Instead, robotic doubles signal only mechanism and artificiality, the lack of any human essence. The debt to *Frankenstein* runs deep. In Ridley Scott's *Blade Runner*, the undertones of nineteenth-century Gothic are never far from the surface of the futuristic dark detective film. Set in a gloomy, ruinous and alienating Los Angeles of the future, the film follows the fortunes of a group of renegade 'replicants', artificial creations virtually indistinguishable from humans, as they try, like Franken-stein's monster, to make their creator, the scientist controlling the Tyrell corporation, accede to their demands for a more human lifespan. The disaffected blade runner, Deckard, whose task is to identify and terminate the replicants, is the parallel subject of the film as it divides sympathies between pursuer and pursued. Caught between blade runner and replicant, human and android, the narrative gradually erodes the differences distinguishing one from the other, leaving doubts that haunt the properly simulated romantic ending of the first version of the film.

Film narratives that establish the Romantic differences between strong, self-sufficient and autonomous individuality and destruc-tive, mechanical and programmed simulations are legion. In the impressive image of Arnold Schwarzenegger, however, the two strands are neatly embodied: in *Conan the Barbarian* the physique is the vehicle for a romance fantasy of the dark ages in which a primordial human bodily and psychological power is imagined; in contrast, the *Terminator* generates human fears of obliteration by a relentlessly determined machinic power. The images of strength and power that are established through the opposition of human and machine draw on the masculine elements of Gothic fiction. In *Alien* (1979) other Gothic associations are brought to the fore. The wrecked alien spaceship and the bleak planet suggest the gloom, ruin and awful desolation of Gothic architecture and landscape. The coded message the spaceship transmits is not a distress signal, but a warning which goes unheeded by the human cargo ship that attends the call. Unaware of the dangers that their employers, another sinister and powerful corporation, have put them in, the crew are unwitting victims of their attempt to secure the power and profit of possessing such an efficient and utterly inhuman killing machine. The horror of the alien lies not only in its lethal power: its parasitical mode of procreation, using human bodies as hosts, means that it is a threat that emerges from within. Indeed, brought aboard inside a member of crew, the alien runs amok. In the cavernous and labyrinthine cargo ship the atmosphere of terror and suspense sustained by the reversible dynamic of hunters and hunted follows Gothic patterns. This is reinforced by the film's focus on a woman, Ripley, who becomes a science fiction Gothic heroine. The strength and self-possession of the heroine, however, distinguishes her from earlier figures, whose faintings and flight signalled the powerlessness of persecuted femininity. Sexual differences, moreover, are presented in the maternal images suggested by the design of the alien 'mother' ship. The vessel is a giant womb, the repository of the eggs that turn into monstrous and destructive progeny. Associations with the conflicting emotions evoked by the mother in 'female Gothic', however, are complicated by the irony of the corporate computer's name, 'Mother': it suggests that the matrix of technology and artificial intelligence has supplanted human figures.

Often reinforcing links between science fiction and Gothic, the cinema has also been the place where the major texts of Gothic writing have been kept alive in popular rather than literary culture. *Frankenstein, Jekyll and Hyde* and *Dracula*, in the many film versions of them that have been made, have spanned the history of the cinema itself. Early films featured Gothic texts: *Frankenstein, The Edison Kinetogram* (1910) adapted Shelley's novel, while scientists and vampires were the focus of German expressionist films like Robert Wiene's *The Cabinet of Dr Caligari* (1920) and Friedrich Murnau's *Nosferatu* (1922) which, with their grotesque villains and stylised sets, played on the gloomy artificiality of Gothic scenes of terror. Other films in this tradition presented modern concerns in very Gothic images. Fritz Lang's *Metropolis* (1926), both visually and narratively, blends old and new in a striking example of modernist Gothic. Angelic heroines, tyrannical fathers and sequences of pursuit through underground tunnels and caverns are combined with a mad scientist who creates a robotic heroine; the gloomy city is divided between a class of industrially roboticised human slaves forced to live a subterranean existence maintaining the awesome machines powering the city, and the rich who enjoy the luxuriously decadent pleasures of the world above. The monstrous and inhuman oppression of one class by another is starkly presented both in the dominating machines that have the terrifying sublimity of Gothic architecture, and in the manufacture of an automated anti-heroine as a sign of the artificiality and deceptiveness of ideological manipulation. Produced in a period when the economic and political systems of Europe were undergoing severe crises, the dark vision of capitalist modes of production and social reproduction are as impressive as the film's romantic ending, in which love wins out over class, is thin.

In the black and white films of Hollywood's discovery of the Gothic in the 1930s, the contrasts are not made on overt class lines. Indeed, the distant world of Europe's past offers curious individuals, villains and monsters that become identified with individual actors: Bela Lugosi and Boris Karloff, themselves strangely European. In James Whale's *Frankenstein* (1931) individual pathology is signalled in the theft of a brain from a laboratory jar marked 'abnormal'. The impressive machines of electrical creation that are located in a Gothic tower give the scientific significance an archaic grandeur. The attempt to win sympathy for a significantly mute monster defers to Shelley's story, a story that is itself used as a frame in Whale's subsequent *Bride of Frankenstein*

(1935) which begins with the ghost story competition told in the 1831 introduction to the novel. The sympathy for the monster is perhaps most heightened in the dramatic end to the first film: an angry torch-bearing mob hunt down the monster. The horror embedded in the mob violence preserves, in a different form from the novel, the uncertain effects of monstrosity on human assumptions and values. It also resonates, in the context of an economically depressed America of the 1930s, with threats of social unrest. Tod Browning's 1932 version of *Dracula* and Rouben Mamoulian's stylish *Dr Jekyll and Mr Hyde* (1932) complete the trio of texts that have formed the Gothic basis of terror and horror cinema in the twentieth century. In these and the many versions that followed certain themes have persisted: the doubleness of identity, the threat and thrill of scientific experimentation, and the violence and insanity that threatens from within and without. In 1950s America, dominated by Cold War anti-communist anxieties, horror became linked to fears about the invasion of both communities and human bodies. Hammer studios in Britain, in the 1960s and 1970s, produced a string of formulaic film horrors inflected by concerns with the social and sexual liberations of the period. Much horror cinema, however, goes well beyond the Gothic form in violence and supernatural suggestiveness, with few points of connection either stylistic or thematic.

Alfred Hitchcock's *Psycho* (1960) brilliantly reworks Gothic extravagance in the creation of mystery, absurdity and menace within the world of the normal and everyday. Sets and scenes, like the gloomy, isolated motel, and the shower curtain stabbing that works like a Gothic veil, are grotesque mirrors for disturbed inner states haunted by the ghostly and dominating figure of the mother. The film's uncanny air of ambivalence displays the psychopath as an object of fear and casts a dark shadow over the limits and effects of normal society and reality.

It is in the spilling over of boundaries, in its uncertain effects on audiences, that Gothic horrors are most disturbing. That these effects are ambivalent, from the eighteenth century onwards, has been signalled by the capacity of Gothic formulae to produce laughter as abundantly as emotions of terror or horror. Stock formulas and themes, when too familiar, are eminently susceptible to parody and self-parody. In the twentieth century this has been continually exploited since Abbot and Costello had fun with the Gothic classics. Cartoons, comic books and comedy series have repeatedly returned to various combinations and amalgamations of figures from texts that seem to merge into one. Television series like *The Addams Family* and *The Munsters,* with their comic inversion of everyday American family life, use a composite of figures from literary and visual Gothic texts. The cult camp musical *The Rocky Horror Show* (1975), bringing Dracula, Frankenstein and the monster together in its collage of stock horror images, parodies both Gothic forms and the horrors associated with them in a celebration of polymorphous sexuality. In the ridiculous artificiality of Gothic figures and rock-and-roll bombast the unnaturalness of all social mores and taboos regarding sexual practices and identities seems to be disclosed.

POSTMODERN GOTHIC

The play of fear and laughter has been inscribed in Gothic texts since their inception, an ambivalence that disturbs critical categories that evaluate their seriousness or triviality. The uncertainty perpetuates Gothic anxieties at the level of narrative and generic form, and affects all categories and boundaries from the generic to the social. Producing powerful emotions rather than aesthetic judgments, effects on audiences and readers rather than instructions for them, narrative forms and devices spill over from worlds of fantasy and fiction into real and social spheres. Exacerbated rather than resolved by the artificial assemblages of Gothic forms, the excess contaminates all distinctions in the way it highlights the function of forms and conventions in the everyday as well as fictional world. The hybrid mixing of forms and narratives has uncanny effects, effects which make narrative play and ambivalence another figure of horror, another duplicitous object to be expelled from proper orders of consciousness and representation.

The twentieth century's escalating anxiety regarding modernity as a combination of civilisation, progress and rationality has become focused on the way that social, historical and individual formations are bound up with the organising effects of narratives. Perceived as a condensation of grand narratives, the legitimacy, universality and unity of modernity is put in question. Part of the challenge to modernity's assumptions, meanings, exclusions and suppressions has emerged in fictions that juxtapose, and thereby reorganise, narrative styles and relations. The stories of Robert Coover's *Pricksongs and Descants* (1969), mixing fragments of myth, fairytale and everyday realism, expose the violence and the violent structures of fantasy that are inscribed in and between the different narratives composing a culture, an uncanny narrative shadow that subverts distinctions between fictional forms and the narratives shaping reality, family and identity. Angela Carter's fiction, self-consciously mixing different forms, including fairytale, legend, science fiction and Gothic, shows the interplay of narratives shaping reality and identity, particularly in relation to the production of meanings for sexuality. Her *Heroes and Villains* (1969) uses the future to reflect on distinctions between civilisation and barbarity. 'The Bloody Chamber' (1979), like the other stories in the collection of the same name, plays with the ways fairytales, legends and Gothic fictions construct identities, fantasies, fears and desires, particularly in terms of female sexuality and desire: a young female speaker casts herself as a Gothic heroine on her marriage to an aristocratic libertine and voluptuary in the Sadeian mould. In echoes of *Rebecca*, the heroine discovers letters of the Marquis's first wife. She turns out to have been a relation of Dracula. Further explorations through the Marquis's precipitously situated castle lead to Radcliffean terrors in dark vaults, amid macabre instruments. Threatened by imminent death at the hands of her husband, a spectral and knightly figure rides to her rescue: the romantic hero is her mother. The play of absurdity and horror interrogates the narrative forms that structure fantasies and have real effects. In her novel *The Infernal Desire Machines of Dr Hoffman* (1972), Carter looks at the play of reality and fantasy by using Freud's notion of the uncanny, but written over the entire social formation. The mysterious villain of the title has stretched the unconscious over the surface of the world so that all perceptions are transformed and mutated along the paths of desire and, more important, the physical laws supposed to govern concrete reality no longer apply. The narrator's picaresque travels through worlds in which conventional distinctions of space and time, matter and spirit, reality and fantasy are irrelevant present different stories, myths and social and scientific principles to suggest that the world is fictional in its broadest sense, an effect of narratives, identifications, fantasies and desires that no longer bow to the grand narrative dominated by the reality principle. Encounters with strange peoples, with different customs, assumptions and attributes, open up singular notions of narrative, reality and identity to heterogeneous possibilities.

Throughout Gothic fiction terror and horror have depended on things not being what they seem. In encouraging superstitious interpretation in, and of, novels by means of narrative devices and generic expectations, Gothic texts have always played along the boundaries between fictional forms and social rules. In the complex assemblage of different stories within early Gothic novels, the labyrinthine complexity ultimately delivers its secret and produces the horror that expels the object of fear, restoring properly conventional boundaries. An uncanny and disturbing uncertainty none the less shadows this process with an ambivalence and duplicity that cannot be contained. In Gothic fictions and films it is this ambivalence and duplicity that has emerged as a distinctly reflexive form of narrative anxiety. It involves a pervasive cultural concern – characterised as postmodernist – that things are not only not what they seem: what they seem is what they are, not a unity of word or image and thing, but words and images without things or as things themselves, effects of narrative form and nothing else. Unstable, unfixed and ungrounded in any reality, truth or identity other than those that narratives provide, there emerges a threat of sublime excess, of a new darkness of multiple and labyrinthine narratives, in which human myths again dissolve, confronted by an uncanny force beyond its control.

The horror of textuality is linked to pervasive terrors of anarchic disintegration or psychotic dissolution. In an impressive example of Gothic fiction, *The Name of the Rose* (1980), Umberto Eco displays its sublimely textual form. With self-consciously Gothic features like the narrative detailing the discovery of a medieval manuscript, the gloomy settings, dark vaults, mysterious deaths and the medieval architecture and history that run through it, the novel rearticulates distinctions between enlightenment rationality and religious superstition. The arrival of a monk, William of Baskerville, and his novice, the narrator, Adso, at a fourteenth-century Abbey dominated by a great octagonal library coincides with a series of mysterious and macabre deaths. Interpreted as signs of divine apocalypse or diabolical machination, the deaths foretell greater terrors for the superstitious monastic community. Baskerville, as his name suggests, has powers of deduction like those of Sherlock Holmes and sets out to provide a rational explanation of supposedly supernatural terrors.

The conventional disingenuity of the 'editor's' preface to the story, stating its absolute distance from concerns of the present, ironically focuses attention on the relation of history and contemporaneity. The novel is full of modern as well as historical allusions: important contemporary antecedents signal a concern with literary and theoretical issues, the writings of Jorge Luis Borges being particularly significant in that the mystery centres on the library constructed in the form of a labyrinth. The novel's mystery is a mystery in and about texts, its object and cause being a text itself, a missing philosophical work whose knowledge and power is feared and desired. Baskerville, monk and detective, is also slightly different from his conventional fictional forebears; his rational and detective skills are presented as critical and analytic abilities: he is an excellent reader of signs and narrative conventions (pp. 24–5). Superstition appears as an effect of misreading, of the mislocation of signs and narratives. Following the clues through the dark corridors and vaults of the Abbey, Baskerville uncovers the textual and fragmented trail of signs and secret codes that both conceal and cause the crimes, arriving at the horror and the explanation in the hidden chamber of the labyrinthine library. The horror is not a bloody spectre or corpse but takes the form of Baskerville's double, an old librarian named Jorge, possessed of religious dogmatism and callous and diabolical cunning, perfect foils for the former's intellectual pride. The murders are explained as the attempt to prevent monks reading a book that was believed lost: Aristotle's second book of the *Poetics*, on comedy. Jorge, to Baskerville's horror, explains the motive for murderous censorship. Such a book by the philosopher would undermine the power of ecclesiastical order by celebrating laughter, legitimating its refusal to respect any law and authority, its rebellious energy threatening the 'dismantling and upsetting of every holy and venerable image' (p. 476). Laughter, activating a diabolical play that exceeds the attempts of sacred horror to expel or control it, is associated with the play of signs, narratives and interpretations, a play that is itself ambivalent in the way it is constructed as either rationally open and liberating or devilishly, anarchically irreverent.

For the order Jorge represents laughter is reviled as the enemy of truth and power. His fear of laughter, however, produces his own acts of irrational and intolerant suppression. The violence that Jorge's dogmatic and restricted order sanctions is, from the narrator's identification with Baskerville's position, shown to be the true object of horror, associated with the superstitious and tyrannical oppression that, throughout Gothic fiction, is linked to the injustice and cruelty of the Catholic Inquisition. Arbitrary, irrational and restrictive power is opposed by Baskerville's enlightened and rational humanism. The invocation of enlightenment values that are produced and contested throughout Gothic fiction is made with a significant difference: truth and reason are no longer seen as absolutes or agents of systems of power. They are, instead, ways of reading in which texts are left open and plural, their play not subjected to a singular, restricted and partial – politically interested – meaning. Adso's concluding reflections remain uncertain about his mentor's motivations and ideas as well as the message that his own manuscript holds. The uncertainty, presented throughout the novel in textual terms, is repeated in a last anecdote of Adso's later return to the Abbey whose library was destroyed in a great conflagration occurring as a result of Jorge's and Baskerville's confrontation. Amid the library's ruins, Adso collects and catalogues some of the tiny fragments of books that remain: 'at the end of my reconstruction, I had before me a kind of lesser library, a symbol of the greater, vanished one: a library made up of fragments, quotations, unfinished sentences, amputated stumps of books' (p. 500).

While *The Name of the Rose* advances this vision of the fragmentary forms of textual, individual and social bodies, whose meanings and identities are effects of patient and partial reconstruction, the image of disintegration that it implies is a shocking one for positions that have been fostered by narratives of individual, social and natural unity, homogeneity and totality. The shadows of narrative duplicity, ambivalence and play that open on to a fragmented glimpse of textuality are, in Alan Parker's film, *Angel Heart* (1986), rendered spectral and threatening objects of terror. Beginning in the manner of a 1950s detective thriller, with a corpse, the film's opening image cedes to an apparently different narrative in which a down-at-heel private eye, Harry Angel, is hired to find a missing person by a mysterious client called Louis Cyphre. The investigation leads Angel away from a grubby New York: it takes him south to a world dominated by religious ritual and voodoo. In the course of the investigation Angel becomes the chief suspect for the murders that shadow it.

Punctuated by flashbacks of mysterious shrouded figures, blood-filled bowls and blood-stained walls, the film suggests another story: one narrative, the detective story, is gradually supplanted by a Faustian tale of diabolical repossession. This is marked by a complete reversal of narrative expectations, a narrative twist that, though characteristic of the detective genre, in this case undermines it. Angel discovers that he is the criminal he has been pursuing. For, in the arcane ritual alluded to in the flashbacks, the heart of an innocent victim, Angel, was torn out and eaten by the criminal who then assumed Angel's appearance. This was done so that the villain could renege on a contract with the devil, substituting another's soul for his own. Satan – 'Lucifer' in the shape and name of 'Louis Cyphre' – returns to claim his due, hiring 'Angel' for the purpose. The word-play reveals the secret of the film, a fact that, in horror, is recognised by 'Angel'. New flashbacks, replicating scenes from earlier in the film, show 'Angel' committing the murders that have shadowed his investigation. The first narrative, it appears, has constructed a false identity: like the shots of mirrors, identity cards and dog tags throughout the film, it is also duplicitous. Angel is detective and criminal, hero and villain, pursuer and pursued, deceiver and dupe. In the play of narrative deceptions bodies, souls, identities and roles are substituted for each other. In the movement between genres there is a diabolical process of deception displayed and performed, a process that multiplies meanings and identities to the point where nothing is what it seems but an effect of narrative appearances. The audience is drawn into this process, duped by the narrative play and robbed of a proper ending and solution to the mystery. The play of narratives is also a game of signs: Louis Cyphre is not only Lucifer, but Lu-cipher, the name that cracks the Faustian narrative's code. The deciphering of the name draws the audience further into the narrative's play of codes, signs and images. The play of words, of codes and ciphers, also encodes the film as a narrative game of ciphers and signs: it is just a matter of word-play. Signs and images are thus presented as diabolical and excluded, cast out in horrified recognition of the empty and superficial word-play that ends the film. Angel, the figure of duplicity, described as the closest thing to 'pure evil', is a transgressor who is simultaneously punished by diabolical law, for breaking the contract, and by secular law, for murder, condemned to burn in hell's flames and the electric chair. Evil, presented in and as a duplicitous play of words, is thus displayed and cast out.

Enmeshed, however, in processes of doubling that its attempt to join its parallel narratives never closes, *Angel Heart*, as a film, as a set of narrative images itself, also signifies the opposite: that identity, meaning and unity are spectral illusions of signs. It cannot expunge this horror, cannot take an external and fixed position. The invocation of evil, however, signals a return to romantic patterns of organising the significance on a global and binary scale. In the films of David Lynch a similar interplay of good and evil, light and dark, is manifested as an uncanny and unavoidable duplicity. In *Blue Velvet* (1986), the play of visual allusions also absorbs the American Gothic tradition in which the uncanny proximity of good and evil is seen to be very close to home, within the boundaries of community life. Lynch's television series, *Twin Peaks* (1990–2), uses similar Gothic contrasts in a visual text whose network of allusions, quotations, stylistic parodies and pastiches was as broad as it was reflexive. Playing with various narrative conventions the series followed the investigation of a terrible murder of a girl in the small-town community to uncover evil's multiple sources in primordial, individual, cultural and narrative locations: deep in the woods, in human fears, selfish desires and sexual repressions, in the community and within the family. The evil in the woods alludes to Hawthorne; the evil father resonates throughout Gothic, as does the identification with psychopathology. The figure of evil, the vagrant face of Bob, appears as the mirror image of the paternal perpetrator, a reflection that haunts the series. Evil, also, is located in outer space, an echo of the Cold War threat of communism that had just disappeared with the collapse of the Soviet Union. Evil's place is multiplied in the dense network of cultural and narrative allusion. Evil is also identified, in the self-conscious use of romance forms, with myths and fictions.

The final battle of good and evil is staged when the detective enters the deceptive Black Lodge – a place of reversals and evil doubles – to save the woman he loves. They both return. But the romantic happy ending is undermined by the final scene. Washing in his hotel bathroom, the detective looks in a mirror. Staring from it is the dishevelled face of Bob, the evil image and sign of diabolical possession. The turning of one into the other, good into evil, forms a doubly self-conscious and banal inversion of the conventional romantic ending. The camera returns from the mirror to focus on the detective's features, now distorted in a malevolent grin that is itself a reflection of the mirror image's evil face. Not so much a conventional display of the truth of interiority, of the evil within, the double reflection presents evil as an effect of images and narrative surfaces, another device of diabolical duplicity. Having turned the figure of good, unity, coherence, identity and cleanliness into evil's double, another alluring figure in a diabolical repertoire of signs, the series' playfulness evokes both laughter and horror: it just plays games, and yet, there seems to be nothing but narrative games, no position outside or determining them, no frame that is not, itself, caught up in a web of duplicity and ambivalent effects that contaminates all cultural boundaries and distinctions.

THE END OF GOTHIC

The much-publicised return of *Dracula* to cinema screens of the 1990s, for all its claims to authenticity, does not evoke the horror capable of expelling the evil, contaminating ambivalence of duplicitous images in which it, too, is enmeshed. Contamination, literal and metaphorical, is a contemporary horror that remains ambivalent in the Gothic of the 1990s. Francis Ford Coppola's *Dracula* (1992) aims at a more authentic rendering of the story, billing itself as 'Bram Stoker's *Dracula*'. The simulation of authenticity is signalled in the reconstruction of Victorian decadence in Dracula's dress, the London settings, the lurid sexual images, the luxuriousness of the Westenra's house and ornamental garden, and in Dr Seward's drug habit. Even Van Helsing's un-characteristic earthiness and appetite for food gives him a less than priestly aura. In the film's magnified shots of blood cells seen through a microscope, the novel's link to diseases of the blood is prominently displayed: the 1990s, like the 1890s, is terrorised by the lethal link between blood and sex, syphilis becoming AIDS. The authenticity of the film's return to images of the past reinforces the link between vampires and sexuality, combining fears in the present with figures from the past. Sexuality, linked to violence and death, again threatens humanity with the sublime and vampiric spectre of its imminent dissolution: both global and microscopic, the threat is simultaneously internal and external, crossing all borders with impunity and uncanny effects. Invading from without and destroying from within, the AIDS virus breaks the cellular defences of individual organisms and leaves its sufferers in an emaciated limbo.

The patterns of repetition and the condition that repetition implies are belied by the film's artificial claims to authenticity. In the frame story to the film the novel's narrative is supplanted by a pseudo-historical account of Vlad the Impaler's tragic love. Dracula is not simply an object of sublime horror. The film also plays down the male bonding so prominent in Stoker's novel and climaxes, not with a hunt delivering the purgative sacrificial violence which restores a patriarchal and domestic order, but where it started, with Mina standing in for Dracula's dead wife in the chapel of the castle: she, rather than Jonathan and Quincey, delivers the cleansing blow that kills him. In Coppola's version Dracula is not coherently or consistently presented as a sublimely imaginary figure of evil, despite the melodramatically demonic dress and the bat costume that seems to be inherited from Batman, another ambivalently Gothic hero. Not entirely an antichrist, vicious aristocrat, bad father or beast, Dracula is less tyrannical and demonic and more victim and sufferer, less libertine and more sentimental romantic hero. The new frame provides the differently divided form in the way it explains his passions and violence as an effect of being tragically robbed of love by the untimely and unnecessary death of his wife. His anger and anguish and the curse he casts on all holy forms cause him to become undead. Bereft of an object of love he preys upon humanity until he sees Harker's miniature of Mina, the very image of his lost love. In the course of the film this is the identity Mina increasingly assumes in her various secret meetings, including dinner, with Dracula. In the final scene Mina kills Dracula in an act of humanitarian mercy and human redemption rather than sacrificial violence, the act taking place in the chapel where, centuries earlier, 'they' were married.

The new frame turns Gothic horror into a sentimental romance. 'Love never dies' was the epigraph to posters advertising the film. 'Bram Stoker's' *Dracula* is merged with another popular romanticisation of a nineteenth-century novel – 'Emily Brontë's' *Wuthering Heights* – as a tale of excessive individual passions, of a love enduring beyond all social forms and history, beyond the grave. Like the end of *Wuthering Heights*, Coppola's film mourns a lost object, a lost story of passion and human, secular love. It does not affirm a unified set of values in a moment of sacred horror and sacrifice like *Dracula*. The vampire is no longer absolutely Other.

In moving from horror to sentimentalism Coppola's film, appropriately enough for the 'caring 1990s', advocates a more humane approach to vampirism, one based on love, tolerance and understanding. Dispensed by and embodied in the figure of woman, these values attempt to replace horror and violence, not so much with laughter and parody but with care and mercy, exemplified by the concerned killing of Dracula.

In the movement between the 1890s and the 1990s, between horror and love, expulsion and tolerance, contradictory and ambivalent impulses disclose radical differences in the relation of one and other, past and present and in the incommensurable narratives in which meaning becomes multiple rather than singular. Human identity and humanist narratives again emerge as duplicitous. Mina, the double of Dracula's wife, assumes that role at the end and thus becomes an adulteress, unfaithful to her other husband, Harker. It is a strange call to monogamy in an age of safe sex. Dracula, as victim and villain, inhuman yet human, is also divided. His love and the love which he inspires in Mina is also violent and passionate and the cause of others' suffering. The doublings of narrative make human stories empty repositories of lost and impassionate signs: in the chapel, the last act of love is surrounded by sacred icons that have become empty symbols, their imaginary power and unity, like Dracula's horror, decomposing in the gap between two narratives. The closure of the film is also emptied of Gothic effect: no climax, no solution, no sacred or rational expulsion of mystery, terror or duplicity. The film's grand themes of individual love and death are haunted by a pervasive sense of loss, the sacred nature of humanity trickling away in empty images and hollow signs: the evanescence of one of modernity's most powerful myths fading like a drawn human face in the sand, erased by tides of different histories and narratives and unable to reconstitute itself. In not repeating the sacrificial violence by which Gothic forms reconstitute a sacred sense of self from the undead and spectral figures of humanist narratives,

Coppola's film mourns an object that is too diffuse and uncertain to be recuperated: it remains, reluctantly, within a play of narratives, between past and present, one and other. Drained of life, a life that in Gothic fiction was always sustained in an ambivalent and textual relation of horror and laughter, sacrificial violence and diabolical play, the romanticism of Coppola's *Dracula* presents its figures of humanity in attenuated and resigned anticipation of an already pervasive absence, undead, perhaps, but not returning. Unable to do anything but half-heartedly tap the last nail in an old coffin, to accidentally squeeze the final stake through the heart of an all-too human figure, the film gently awaits a merciful release from the uncertainties, accidents and excesses of forms whose multiplicity and mobility seem imponderable and meaningless.

With Coppola's *Dracula*, then, Gothic dies, divested of its excesses, of its transgressions, horrors and diabolical laughter, of its brilliant gloom and rich darkness, of its artificial and suggestive forms. Dying, of course, might just be the prelude to other spectral returns.

SELECT BIBLIOGRAPHY

TEXTS

Ainsworth, William Harrison, *The Lancashire Witches* (1849), London, Granada, 1980.

Anonymous, 'Terrorist Novel Writing', *Spirit of the Public Journals* 1 (1797): 227–9.

Austen, Jane, *Northanger Abbey* (1818), ed. Henry Ehrenpreis, Harmondsworth, Penguin, 1985.

Baillie, John, *An Essay on the Sublime* (1747), Augustan Reprint Society 43, University of California, 1953.

Baldick, Chris (ed.), *The Oxford Book of Gothic Tales*, Oxford, Oxford University Press, 1992.

Barbauld, Anna Laetitia, *The Works of Anna Laetitia Barbauld*, 2 vols, London, Longman, 1825.

Beattie, James, *On Fable and Romance* (1783), in *Novel and Romance: A Documentary Record 1700–1800*, ed. Ioan Williams, London, Routledge & Kegan Paul, 1970, pp. 309–27.

Beckford, William, *Vathek* (1786), ed. Roger Lonsdale, Oxford, Oxford University Press, 1983.

Bierce, Ambrose, *Can Such Things Be?*, London, Jonathan Cape, 1926.

———, *In the Midst of Life*, New Jersey, Citadel Press, 1946.

Blackwood, Algernon, *Ancient Sorceries and Other Stories*, Harmondsworth, Penguin, 1968.

Blair, Hugh, *Lectures on Rhetoric and Belles Lettres* (1783), 6th edn, 3 vols, London, Strachan & Cadell, 1796.

Blair, Robert, *The Grave* (1743), Los Angeles, Augustan Reprint Society, 1973.

Braddon, Mary Elizabeth, 'Good Lady Ducayne', *Strand Magazine* 11 (1896): 185–99.

Brockden Brown, Charles, *Wieland and Memoirs of Carwin the Biloquist* (1798), ed. Jay Fliegelman, Harmondsworth, Penguin, 1991.

Brontë, Charlotte, *Jane Eyre* (1847), ed. Q. D. Leavis, Harmondsworth, Penguin, 1966.

——, *Villette* (1853), ed. Sandra Kemp, London, Dent, 1993.

Brontë, Emily, *Wuthering Heights* (1847), ed. Ian Jack, Oxford, Oxford University Press, 1981.

Bulwer-Lytton, Edward, *Zanoni: A Rosicrucian Tale* (1842), New York, Garland, 1970.

——, 'The Haunters and the Haunted: or the House and the Brain' (1859), in *Great Tales of Terror and the Supernatural*, ed. Herbert A. Wise and Phyllis Fraser, New York, Random House, 1947.

Burke, Edmund, *A Philosophical Enquiry into Our Ideas of the Sublime and the Beautiful* (1757), ed. Adam Phillips, Oxford, Oxford University Press, 1990.

——, *Reflections on the Revolution in France* (1790), ed. Conor Cruise O'Brien, Harmondsworth, Penguin, 1969.

Carpenter, Edward, *Civilisation*, London, Swan Sonnenschein, 1889.

Carter, Angela, *Heroes and Villains* (1969), Harmondsworth, Penguin, 1972.

——, *The Infernal Desire Machines of Dr Hoffman* (1972), Harmondsworth, Penguin, 1982.

——, *The Bloody Chamber and Other Stories* (1979), Harmondsworth, Penguin, 1981.

Cleland, John, 'Review of *Peregrine Pickle*', *Monthly Review* 4 (Mar. 1751), in *Novel and Romance: A Documentary Record 1700–1800*, ed. Ioan Williams, London, Routledge & Kegan Paul, 1970, pp. 160–2.

Cobbe, Frances Power, 'Unconscious Cerebration', *Macmillan's Magazine* 23 (Nov. 1870): 24–37.

Coleridge, S. T., 'Review of *The Mysteries of Udolpho*', *Critical Review* (Second Series) 11 (Aug. 1794): 361–72.

—— , 'Review of *The Monk*', *Critical Review* (Second Series) 19 (Feb. 1796): 194–200.

Collins, Wilkie, *The Woman in White* (1860), ed. Harvey Peter Sucksmith, Oxford, Oxford University Press, 1980.

Conrad, Joseph, *Heart of Darkness* (1902), ed. Paul O'Prey, Harmondsworth, Penguin, 1973.

—— , *The Secret Agent: A Simple Tale* (1907), ed. Martin Seymour-Smith, Harmondsworth, Penguin, 1963.

Coover, Robert, *Pricksongs and Descants*, New York, E. P. Dutton, 1969.

Cox, Jeffrey N. (ed.), *Seven Gothic Dramas 1789–1825*, Athens, Ohio University Press, 1992.

Cox, Michael and Gilbert, R. A. (eds), *Victorian Ghost Stories*, Oxford, Oxford University Press, 1992.

Dacre, Charlotte, *Zofloya; or, the Moor* (1806), 3 vols, New York, Arno Press, 1974.

Dickens, Charles, *Oliver Twist* (1838), ed. Peter Fairclough, Harmondsworth, Penguin, 1966.

—— , *Bleak House* (1853), ed. Norman Page, Harmondsworth, Penguin, 1985.

——, *Hard Times* (1854), ed. David Craig, Harmondsworth, Penguin, 1969.

——, *Little Dorrit* (1855), ed. John Holloway, Harmondsworth, Penguin, 1967.

——, *Great Expectations* (1860–1), ed. Angus Calder, Harmondsworth, Penguin, 1985.

Dinesen, Isak, *Seven Gothic Tales* (1934), Harmondsworth, Penguin, 1963.

du Maurier, Daphne, *Rebecca* (1938), New York, Doubleday, 1948.

Eco, Umberto, *The Name of the Rose* (1980), trans. William Weaver, London, Pan, 1984.

Eliot, George, 'The Lifted Veil' (1859), in *Silas Marner, The Lifted Veil and Brother Jacob*, Oxford, Oxford University Press, 1940.

Faulkner, William, *The Sound and the Fury* (1931), Harmondsworth, Penguin, 1964.

——, *Absalom, Absalom!* (1936), Harmondsworth, Penguin, 1971.

Flammenberg, Lawrence, *The Necromancer; or the Tale of the Black Forest* (1794), trans. Peter Teuthold, London, Folio Press, 1968.

Frayling, Christopher (ed.), *Vampyres: Lord Byron to Count Dracula*, London, Faber & Faber, 1991.

Gaskell, Elizabeth, *Mrs Gaskell's Tales of Mystery and Horror*, ed. Michael Ashley, London, Victor Gollancz, 1978.

Gibson, William, *Necromancer* (1984), London, Grafton, 1986.

Gilman, Charlotte Perkins, *The Yellow Wallpaper* (1892), London, Virago, 1992.

Godwin, William, *Enquiry Concerning Political Justice* (1793), ed. Isaac Kramnick, Harmondsworth, Penguin, 1985.

——, *Caleb Williams* (1794), ed. Maurice Hindle, Harmondsworth, Penguin, 1988.

——, *St Leon* (1799), ed. Pamela Clemit, *Collected Novels and Memoirs of William Godwin*, vol. 4, London, Pickering, 1992.

Grosse, Carl, *Horrid Mysteries: A Story* (1797), trans. Peter Will, London, Folio Press, 1968.

Hawthorne, Nathaniel, *Young Goodman Brown and Other Tales*, ed. Brian Harding, Oxford, Oxford University Press, 1987.

——, *The Scarlet Letter* (1850), London, Dent, 1906.

——, *The House of Seven Gables* (1851), ed. Michael Davitt Bell, Oxford, Oxford University Press, 1991.

——, *The Marble Faun* (1860), New York, Pocket Books, 1958.

Hoffman, E. T. A., *The Golden Pot and Other Tales*, trans. Ritchie Robertson, Oxford, Oxford University Press, 1992.

Hogg, James, *The Private Memoirs and Confessions of a Justified Sinner* (1824), London, Cresset Press, 1947.

Horsley-Curties, T. J., *The Monk of Udolpho: A Romance* (1807), 4 vols, New York, Arno Press, 1977.

Hurd, Richard, *Letters on Chivalry and Romance* (1762), Augustan Reprint Society 101–2, University of California, 1963.

James, Henry, *The Ghostly Tales of Henry James*, ed. Leon Edel, New Brunswick, NJ, Rutgers University Press, 1948.

——, 'Mary Elizabeth Braddon' (1865), *Literary Criticism*, ed. Leon Edel, New York, The Library of America, 1984.

James, M. R., *Casting the Runes and other Ghost Stories*, ed. Michael Cox, Oxford, Oxford University Press, 1987.

Johnson, Samuel, *The Rambler* 4 (1750), *Samuel Johnson*, ed. Donald Greene, Oxford, Oxford University Press, 1986, pp. 175–9.

Kafka, Franz, *Metamorphosis and Other Stories*, trans. Willa and Edwin Muir, Harmondsworth, Penguin, 1961.

——, *The Trial* (1925), trans. Willa and Edwin Muir, London, Heron, 1968.

——, *The Castle* (1926), trans. Willa and Edwin Muir, Harmondsworth, Penguin, 1957.

Kames, Henry Home, Lord, *Elements of Criticism* (1762), 11th edn, London, B. Blake, 1839.

Le Fanu, J. Sheridan, *In a Glass Darkly* (1872), Gloucester, Alan Sutton Publishing, 1990.

Lee, Sophia, *The Recess: or, A Tale of Other Times* (1783–5), 3 vols, New York Arno Press, 1972.

Lewis, Matthew, Gregory, *The Monk* (1796), ed. Howard Anderson, Oxford, Oxford University Press, 1980.

——, *The Castle Spectre: A Drama* (1797), Oxford, Woodstock Books, 1990.

Lovecraft, H. P. and Derleth, August, *The Lurker at the Threshold* (1945), London, Victor Gollancz, 1989.

Machen, Arthur, *The Great God Pan*, London, John Lane, 1894.

——, *The Three Imposters*, London, John Lane, 1895.

Macpherson, James, *The Poems of Ossian* (1762), Edinburgh, Geddes, 1896.

Mallett, Paul-Henri, *Northern Antiquities* (1770), trans. Thomas Percy, ed. I. A. Blackwell, London, Bohn's Library, 1847.

Matthias, T. J., *The Pursuits of Literature* (1796), 13th edn, London, T. Becket, 1805.

Maturin, Charles Robert, *The Milesian Chief* (1812), ed. Robert Lee Worff, New York, Garland, 1979.

—— , *Bertram, or, the Castle of Aldobrand* (1816), Oxford, Woodstock Books, 1992.

—— , *Melmoth the Wanderer: A Tale* (1820), ed. Douglas Grant, Oxford, Oxford University Press, 1989.

Morris, William, *The Early Romances of William Morris in Prose and Verse*, London, Dent, 1907.

Morrison, Toni, *Beloved* (1987), London, Picador, 1988.

O'Connor, Flannery, *Everything that Rises Must Converge*, Harmondsworth, Penguin, 1975.

Paine, Thomas, *The Rights of Man* (1791–2), *The Thomas Paine Reader*, ed. Michael Foot and Isaac Kramnick, Harmondsworth, Penguin, 1987.

Peacock, Thomas Love, *Nightmare Abbey* (1817–18) and *Crotchet Castle* (1831), ed. Raymond Wright, Harmondsworth, Penguin, 1986.

Peake, Mervyn, *Gormenghast* (1950), Harmondsworth, Penguin, 1969.

Peake, R. B., *Presumption; or, The Fate of Frankenstein* (1823), in Steven Earl Forry, *Hideous Progenies*, Philadelphia, University of Pennsylvania Press, 1990.

Percy, Thomas, *Reliques of Ancient English Poetry* (1765), 3 vols, ed. Henry B. Wheatley, New York, Dover Publications, 1966.

Poe, Edgar Allan, *Selected Writings*, ed. David Galloway, Harmondsworth, Penguin, 1967.

Polidori, John, 'The Vampyre: A Tale', in *Three Gothic Novels*, ed. E. F. Bleiler, New York, Dover Publications, 1966.

Radcliffe, Ann, *A Sicilian Romance* (1790), ed. Alison Milbank, Oxford, Oxford University Press, 1993.

—— , *The Romance of the Forest* (1791), ed. Chloe Chard, Oxford, Oxford University Press, 1986.

—— , *The Mysteries of Udolpho* (1794), ed. Bonamy Dobree, Oxford, Oxford University Press, 1980.

—— , *The Italian, or the Confessional of the Black Penitents* (1797), ed. Frederick Garber, Oxford, Oxford University Press, 1981.

—— , 'On the Supernatural in Poetry', *New Monthly Magazine* 16 (1826): 145–52.

Reeve, Clara, *The Old English Baron: A Gothic Story* (1778), ed. James Trainer, Oxford, Oxford University Press, 1977.

—— , *The Progress of Romance* (1785), 2 vols, New York, Garland, 1970.

Review of *Frankenstein*, *Edinburgh (Scot's) Magazine* (Second Series) 2 (Mar. 1818): 249–53.

Review of *Melmoth*, *Monthly Review* xciv (1821): 81–90.

Review of *The Monk*, *British Critic* 7 (Jun. 1796): 677.

Review of *The Monk*, *Analytical Review* 24 (Oct. 1796): 403–4.

Review of *The Monk*, *Monthly Review* (New Series) 23 (Aug. 1797): 451.

Review of *The Mysteries of Udolpho*, *European Magazine* 25 (Jun. 1794): 433–40.

Review of *The Mysteries of Udolpho*, *British Critic* 4 (Aug. 1794): 110–21.

Review of *The Mysteries of Udolpho*, *Gentleman's Magazine* 64 (Sept. 1794): 834.

Review of *The Mysteries of Udolpho*, *Monthly Review* (New Series) 15 (Nov. 1794): 278–83.

Reynolds, G. W., *The Mysteries of London* (1848), 2 vols, New York, AMS Press, 1989.

Rider Haggard, H., *She* (1886), Oxford, Oxford University Press, 1991.

Roche, Regina Maria, *The Children of the Abbey: A Tale* (1794), 4 vols, London, Minerva, 1810.

—— , *Clermont: A Tale* (1798), 4 vols, London, Folio Press, 1968.

Row, T., 'Letter to the Editor', *Gentleman's Magazine* 37 (Dec. 1767), in *Novel and Romance: A Documentary Record 1700–1800*, ed. Ioan Williams, London, Routledge & Kegan Paul, 1970, pp. 272–3.

Ruskin, John, *The Stones of Venice*, 3 vols, London, George Allen, 1905.

Sade, D. A. F., Marquis de, 'Reflections on the Novel', in *One Hundred and Twenty Days of Sodom*, trans. Austryn Wainhouse and Richard Seaver, London, Arrow Books, 1989, pp. 91–116.

Scott, Walter, *Waverley* (1814), ed. Claire Lamont, Oxford, Clarendon, 1981.

—— , 'Review of *Frankenstein*', *Blackwood's Edinburgh Magazine* 2 (Mar. 1818): 613–20.

—— , *The Bride of Lammermoor* (1819), ed. Fiona Robertson, Oxford, Oxford University Press, 1991.

Shelley, Mary, *Frankenstein; or, the Modern Prometheus* (1831), ed. M. K. Joseph, Oxford, Oxford University Press, 1969.

Shelley, Percy Bysshe, *Zastrozzi* (1810) and *St Irvyne* (1811), ed. Stephen C. Behrendt, Oxford, Oxford University Press, 1986.

Stevenson, Robert Louis, *The Strange Case of Dr Jekyll and Mr Hyde and Other Stories*, ed. Jenni Calder, Harmondsworth, Penguin, 1979.

Stoker, Bram, *Dracula* (1897), ed. Maurice Hindle, Harmondsworth, Penguin, 1993.

Summers, Montague (ed.), *The Supernatural Omnibus*, London, Victor Gollancz, 1949.

Tales of the Dead (1813), ed. Terry Hale, Chislehurst, The Gothic Society, 1992.

Thompson, G. Richard (ed.), *Romantic Gothic Tales 1790–1840*, New York, Harper & Row, 1979.

Walpole, Horace, *The Castle of Otranto: A Gothic Story* (1764), ed. W. S. Lewis, Oxford, Oxford University Press, 1982.

——— , *The Yale Edition of Horace Walpole's Correspondence*, ed. W. S. Lewis and A. Dayle Wallace, New Haven, Conn. and London, Yale University Press, 1937.

Warton, Thomas, *History of English Poetry from the Twelfth to the Close of the Sixteenth Century* (1774–81), 4 vols, ed. W. Carew Hazlitt (1871), New York, Haskell House Publishers, 1979.

Wells, H. G., *The Island of Dr Moreau* (1896), London, Heinemann, 1921.

——— , *The War of the Worlds* (1898), London, Heinemann, 1951.

Wilde, Oscar, *The Picture of Dorian Gray* (1891), ed. Peter Ackroyd, Harmondsworth, Penguin, 1985.

Williams, Ioan, (ed.) *Novel and Romance: A Documentary Record 1700–1800*, London, Routledge & Kegan Paul, 1970.

Wollstonecraft, Mary, *A Vindication of the Rights of Men* (1790), in *The Works of Mary Wollstonecraft*, vol. 5, ed. Janet Todd and Marilyn Butler, London, Pickering, 1989.

Young, Edward, *Night Thoughts* (1749–51), ed. Stephen Cornford, Cambridge, Cambridge University Press, 1989.

CRITICISM

Abraham, N., 'Notes on the Phantom: A Complement to Freud's Metapsychology', *Critical Inquiry* 13 (1987): 287–92.

Aguirre, Manuel, *The Closed Space: Horror Literature and Western Symbolism*, Manchester, Manchester University Press, 1990.

Alexander, Christine, '"That Kingdom of Gloom": Charlotte Brontë, the Annuals and the Gothic', *Nineteenth-Century Literature* 47 (1993): 409–38.

Ames, Dianne S., 'Strawberry Hill: Architecture of the "as if"', *Studies in Eighteenth-Century Culture* 8 (1979): 351–63.

Auerbach, Jonathan, 'Poe's Other Double: The Reader in the Fiction', *Criticism* 24 (1982): 341–61.

Baldick, Chris, *In Frankenstein's Shadow: Myth Monstrosity and Nineteenth-Century Writing*, Oxford, Clarendon, 1987.

Barthes, Roland, 'Textual Analysis of Poe's "Valdemar"', in *Modern Criticism and Theory: A Reader*, ed. David Lodge, London, Longman, 1988, pp. 173–95.

Bataille, Georges, *Literature and Evil* (1957), trans. Alastair Hamilton, London, Marion Boyars, 1973.

Baudrillard, Jean, *The Transparency of Evil* (1990), trans. James Benedict, London, Verso, 1993.

Bayer-Berenbaum, Linda, *The Gothic Imagination: Expansion in Gothic Literature and Art*, London and Toronto, Associated University Presses, 1982.

Beer, Gillian, '"Our Unnatural No-Voice": The Heroic Epistle, Pope and Women's Gothic', *Yearbook of English Studies* 12 (1982): 125–51.

Birkhead, Edith, *The Tale of Terror: A Study of the Gothic Romance*, London, Constable, 1921.

Brantlinger, Patrick, 'Imperial Gothic: Atavism and the Occult in the British Adventure Novel, 1880–1914', *English Literature in Transition (1880–1920)* 28 (1985): 243–52.

Briggs, Julia, *Night Visitors: The Rise and Fall of the English Ghost Story*, London, Faber & Faber, 1977.

Bronfen, Elisabeth, *Over Her Dead Body: Death, Femininity and the Aesthetic*, Manchester, Manchester University Press, 1992.

Brooks, Peter, 'Virtue and Terror: *The Monk*', *English Literary History* 40 (1973): 249–63.

Brophy, Philip, 'Horrality – the Textuality of Contemporary Horror Films', *Screen* 27 (1987): 11–25.

Brown, Marshall, 'A Philosophical View of the Gothic Novel', *Studies in Romanticism* 26 (1987): 275–301.

Butler, Marilyn, *Romantic, Rebels and Reactionaries: English Literature and Its Background 1760–1830*, Oxford, Oxford University Press, 1981.

Carroll, Noel, *The Philosophy of Horror or Paradoxes of the Heart*, London, Routledge, 1990.

Castle, Terry, 'The Spectralization of the Other in *The Mysteries of Udolpho*', in *The New Eighteenth Century*, ed. Laura Brown and Felicity Nussbaum, London, Methuen, 1987.

Clark, Kenneth, *The Gothic Revival: An Essay in the History of Taste* (1928), 3rd edn, London, John Murray, 1962.

Clery, E. J., 'The Politics of the Gothic Heroine in the 1790s', in *Reviewing Romanticism*, ed. Philip W. Martin and Robin Jarvis, London and Basingstoke, Macmillan, 1992, pp. 69–85.

Coates, J. D., 'Techniques of Terror in *The Woman in White*', *Durham University Journal* 73 (1981): 177–89.

Cooke, Arthur, 'Some Side Lights on the Theory of Gothic Romance', *Modern Language Quarterly* 12 (1951): 429–36.

Cottom, Daniel, *The Civilized Imagination: A Study of Ann Radcliffe, Jane Austen, and Sir Walter Scott*, Cambridge, Cambridge University Press, 1985.

Craft, Christopher, '"Kiss Me with Those Red Lips": Gender and Inversion in Bram Stoker's *Dracula*', *Representations* 8 (1984): 107–33.

Creed, Barbara, 'Horror and Monstrous-Feminine: An Imaginary Abjection', *Screen* 27 (1986): 44–71.

Dahl, Curtis, 'Bulwer-Lytton and the School of Catastrophe', *Philological Quarterly* 32 (1953): 428–42.

Dekker, George, *The American Historical Romance*, Cambridge, Cambridge University Press, 1987.

Derrida, Jacques, 'The Purveyor of Truth', *Yale French Studies* 52 (1975): 31–113.

Doody, Margaret A., 'Deserts, Ruins, Troubled Waters: Female Dreams in Fiction and the Development of the Gothic Novel', *Genre* 10 (1977): 529–72.

Durant, David, 'Ann Radcliffe and the Conservative Gothic', *Studies in English Literature 1500–1900* 22 (1982): 519–30.

Eggenschwiler, David, '*Melmoth the Wanderer*: Gothic on Gothic', *Genre* 8 (1975): 165–81.

Eigner, Edwin M., *The Metaphysical Novel in England and America: Dickens, Bulwer, Melville, and Hawthorne*, Berkeley, University of California Press, 1978.

Ellis, Kate Ferguson, *The Contested Castle: Gothic Novels and the Subversion of Domestic Ideology*, Urbana and Chicago, University of Illinois Press, 1987.

Fiedler, Leslie, *Love and Death in the American Novel*, New York, Stein & Day, 1966.

Fleenor, Juliann E. (ed.), *The Female Gothic*, Montreal, Eden Press, 1983.

Foucault, Michel, 'Language to Infinity', in *Language, Counter-Memory, Practice*, trans. Donald F. Bouchard and Sherry Simon, Oxford, Blackwell, 1977.

—— , 'The Eye of Power', in *Power/Knowledge*, trans. Colin Gordon *et al.*, Brighton, Harvester, 1980, pp. 146–65.

Fowler, Kathleen, 'Hieroglyphics of Fire: *Melmoth the Wanderer*', *Studies in Romanticism* 25 (1986): 521–39.

Frank, Frederick S., *Gothic Fiction: A Master List of Twentieth-Century Criticism and Research*, London, Meckler, 1988.

Freud, Sigmund, 'The Uncanny' (1919), in *Standard Edition of the Complete Psychological Works*, vol. 17, trans. James Strachey, London, Hogarth Press, 1955, pp. 218–56.

Frye, Northrop, *The Secular Scripture: A Study of the Structure of Romance*, Cambridge, Mass. and London, Harvard University Press, 1976.

Gordon, Jan B., 'Narrative Enclosure as Textual Ruin: An Archaeology of Gothic Consciousness', *Dickens Studies Annual* 11 (1983): 209–38.

Graham, Kenneth W. (ed.), *Gothic Fictions: Prohibition/Transgression*, New York, AMS Press, 1989.

—— , (ed.), *Vathek and the Escape from Time*, New York, AMS Press, 1990.

Griffith, Clark, 'Poe and the Gothic', in *Papers on Poe*, ed. Richard P. Veler, Ohio, Chantry Music Press, 1972, pp. 21–7.

Grixti, Joseph, *Terrors of Uncertainty: The Cultural Contexts of Horror Fiction*, London, Routledge, 1989.

Guest, Harriet, 'The Wanton Muse: Politics and Gender in Gothic Theory after 1760', in *Beyond Romanticism*, ed. Stephen Copley and John Whale, London, Routledge, 1992.

Haggerty, George E., 'Fact and Fantasy in the Gothic Novel', *Nineteenth-Century Fiction* 39 (1985): 379–91.

Harries, Elizabeth W., 'Duplication and Duplicity: James Hogg's *Private Memoirs and Confessions of a Justified Sinner*', *Wordsworth Circle* 10 (1979): 187–96.

Heath, Stephen, 'Psychopathia Sexualis: Stevenson's Strange Case', *Critical Quarterly* 28 (1986): 93–108.

Heller, Tamar, *Dead Secrets: Wilkie Collins and the Female Gothic*, New Haven, Conn. and London, Yale University Press, 1992.

Hogle, Jerrold E., 'The Texture of Self in Godwin's *Things As They Are*', *Boundary* 7 (1979): 261–81.

—— , 'Otherness in *Frankenstein*: The Confinement/Autonomy of Fabrication', *Structuralist Review* 2 (1980): 20–48.

—— , 'The Restless Labyrinth: Cryptonomy in the Gothic Novel', *Arizona Quarterly* 36 (1980): 330–58.

Howells, Coral Ann, *Love, Mystery and Misery: Feeling in Gothic Fiction*, London, Athlone Press, 1978.

—— , 'The Gothic Way of Death in English Fiction 1790–1820', *British Journal for Eighteenth-Century Studies* 5 (1982): 207–15.

Hume, Robert D., 'Gothic versus Romantic: A Re-evaluation of the Gothic Novel', *PMLA* 84 (1969): 282–90.

Jackson, Rosemary, 'The Silenced Text: Shades of Gothic in Victorian Fiction', *Minnesota Review* 13 (1979): 98–112.

—— , *Fantasy: The Literature of Subversion*, London, Methuen, 1981.

Jarrett, David, 'The Fall of the House of Clennam: Gothic Conventions in *Little Dorrit*', *Dickensian* 73 (1977): 155–61.

Kahane, Claire, 'Gothic Mirrors and Feminine Identity', *Centennial Review* 24 (1980): 43–64.

Kaufman, Pamela, 'Burke, Freud, and the Gothic', *Studies in Burke and His Time* 13 (1972): 2178–92.

Kiely, Robert, *The Romantic Novel in England*, Cambridge, Mass., Harvard University Press, 1972.

Kliger, Samuel, *The Goths in England: A Study in Seventeenth and Eighteenth Century Thought*, Cambridge, Mass., Harvard University Press, 1952.

Knoff, C. R., '*Caleb Williams* and the Attack on Romance', *Studies in the Novel* 8 (1976): 81–7.

Kristeva, Julia, *Powers of Horror: An Essay on Abjection*, trans. Leon S. Roudiez, New York, Columbia University Press, 1982.

Lacan, Jacques, 'Seminar on "The Purloined Letter"', *Yale French Studies* 48 (1972): 38–72.

Leps, Marie-Christine, *Apprehending the Criminal: The Production of Deviance in Nineteenth-Century Discourse*, Durham, NC and London, Duke University Press, 1992.

Levine, George, and Knoepflmacher, U. C., *The Endurance of Frankenstein: Essays on Mary Shelley's Novel*, Berkeley, University of California Press, 1979.

Longueil, Alfred E., 'The Word "Gothic" in Eighteenth-Century Criticism', *Modern Language Notes* 38 (1923): 453–6.

Lovejoy, Arthur O., *Essays in the History of Ideas*, Baltimore and London, Johns Hopkins University Press, 1948.

Lovell, Terry, *Consuming Fiction*, London, Verso, 1987.

Lyndenburg, Robin, 'Gothic Architecture and Fiction: A Survey of Critical Responses', *Centennial Review* 22 (1978): 95–109.

——— , 'Ghostly Rhetoric: Ambivalence in M. G. Lewis' *The Monk*', *Ariel* 10 (1979): 65–79.

Lyotard, Jean-Francois, 'Answering the Question: What is Postmodernism?', trans. Regis Durand, in *The Postmodern Condition: A Report on Knowledge*, Manchester, Manchester University Press, 1984, pp. 71–82.

McInerney, Peter, 'Satanic Conceits in *Frankenstein* and *Wuthering Heights*', *Milton and the Romantics* 4 (1980): 1–15.

McIntyre, C., 'Were the "Gothic Novels" Gothic?', *PMLA* 36 (1921): 644–7.

McNutt, D. J., *The Eighteenth-Century Gothic Novel: An Annotated Bibliography of Criticism and Selected Texts*, New York, Garland, 1975.

Madoff, Mark, 'The Useful Myth of Gothic Ancestry', *Studies in Eighteenth Century Culture* 8 (1979): 337–50.

Masse, Michelle A., *In the Name of Love: Women, Masochism and the Gothic*, Ithaca and London, Cornell University Press, 1992.

Mayo, Robert D., 'The Gothic Short Story in the Magazines', *Modern Language Review* 37 (1942): 448–54.

——— , 'Gothic Romance in the Magazines', *PMLA* 65 (1950): 762–89.

Maxwell, Richard C., 'G. M. Reynolds, Dickens and *The Mysteries of London*', *Nineteenth-Century Fiction* 32 (1977): 188–213.

Mercer, Kobena, 'Monster Metaphors: Notes on Michael Jackson's "Thriller"', *Screen* 27 (1986): 26–43.

Miles, Robert, *Gothic Writing 1750–1820*, London, Routledge, 1993.

Miller, Jacqueline T., 'The Imperfect Tale: Articulation, Rhetoric and Self in *Caleb Williams*', *Criticism* 20 (1978): 366–82.

Miyoshi, Masao, *The Divided Self: A Perspective on the Literature of the Victorians*, London, University of London Press, 1969.

Moers, Ellen, *Literary Women*, London, W. H. Allen, 1978.

Monk, Samuel Holt, *The Sublime: A Study of Critical Theories in XVIII-Century England*, Ann Arbor, University of Michigan Press, 1960.

Moretti, Franco, *Signs Taken for Wonders: Essays on the Sociology of Literary Forms*, trans. Susan Fischer, David Forgacs and David Miller, London, Verso, 1983.

Morris, D. B., 'Gothic Sublimity', *New Literary History* 16 (1985): 299–319.

Napier, Elizabeth, *The Failure of Gothic: Problems of Disjunction in an Eighteenth-Century Literary Form*, Oxford, Clarendon, 1987.

Nelson, Lowry Jr, 'Night Thoughts on the Gothic Novel', *Yale Review* 52 (1962): 236–57.

Nicholson, Marjorie Hope, *Mountain Gloom and Mountain Glory: The Development of the Aesthetics of the Infinite* (1959), New York, Norton, 1963.

Nietzsche, Friedrich, *Beyond Good and Evil* (1886), in *Basic Writings of Nietzsche*, trans. Walter Kaufmann, New York, Random House, 1968.

Novak, Maximilian E., 'Gothic Fiction and the Grotesque', *Novel* 13 (1979): 50–67.

Paulson, Ronald, *Representations of Revolution (1789–1820)*, New Haven, Conn. and London, Yale University Press, 1983.

Philmus, Robert M., *Into the Unknown: The Evolution of Science Fiction*

from Francis Godwin to H. G. Wells, Berkeley, University of
California Press, 1970.

Pick, Daniel, '"Terrors of the Night": Dracula and "Degeneration"
in the Late Nineteenth Century', *Critical Quarterly* 30 (1984): 71–87.

Platzner, Robert L., 'Gothic versus Romantic: A Rejoinder', *PMLA* 86
(1971): 266–74.

Poovey, Mary, 'Ideology in *The Mysteries of Udolpho*', *Criticism* 21 (1979):
307–30.

Poteet, Lewis J., '*Dorian Gray* and the Gothic Novel', *Modern Fiction
Studies* 17 (1971): 239–48.

Prawer, S. S., *Caligari's Children: The Film as Tale of Terror*, Oxford, Oxford
University Press, 1980.

Praz, Mario, *The Romantic Agony* (1933), trans. Angus Davidson, Oxford,
Oxford University Press, 1970.

Punter, David, *The Literature of Terror: A History of Gothic Fiction from
1765 to the Present Day*, London, Longman, 1980.

Railo, Eino, *The Haunted Castle: A Study of the Elements of English
Romanticism*, London, George Routledge & Sons, 1927.

Rome, Joy, 'Twentieth-Century Gothic: Mervyn Peake's *Gormenghast*
Trilogy', *Unisa English Studies* 12 (1974): 42–54.

Sadleir, Michael, *The Northanger Novels: A Footnote to Jane Austen*,
Oxford, Oxford University Press, 1927.

Sage, Victor, *Horror Fiction in the Protestant Tradition*, London and
Basingstoke, Macmillan, 1988.

Saposnik, Irving S., 'The Anatomy of *Dr Jekyll and Mr Hyde*', *Studies in
English Literature* 11 (1971): 715–31.

Schroeder, Natalie, '*The Mysteries of Udolpho* and *Clermont*: The

Radcliffean Encroachment on the Art of Regina Maria Roche', *Studies in the Novel* 12 (1980): 131–43.

Sedgwick, Eve Kosofsky, *The Coherence of Gothic Conventions* (1980), London, Methuen, 1986.

—— , *Between Men: English Literature and Male Homosocial Desire*, New York, Columbia University Press, 1985.

Showalter, Elaine, 'American Female Gothic', in *Sister's Choice*, Oxford, Clarendon, 1991.

—— , *Sexual Anarchy: Gender and Culture at the Fin de Siècle*, London, Virago, 1992.

Spector, Robert D., *The English Gothic: A Bibliographic Guide to Writers from Horace Walpole to Mary Shelley*, Westport, Conn., Greenwood Press, 1984.

Spencer, Kathleen L., 'Purity and Danger: *Dracula*, the Urban Gothic, and the Late Victorian Degeneracy Crisis', *English Literary History* 59 (1992): 197–225.

Spivak, Gayatri Chakravorty, 'Three Women's Texts and a Critique of Imperialism', *Critical Inquiry* 12 (1985): 243–61.

Summers, Montague, *The Gothic Quest: A History of the Gothic Novel* (1938), New York, Russell & Russell, 1964.

Thompson, G. R., 'Poe and "Romantic Irony"' in *Papers on Poe*, ed. Richard P. Veler, Ohio, Chantry Music Press, 1972, pp. 28–41.

—— (ed.), *The Gothic Imagination: Essays in Dark Romanticism*, Pullman, Washington University Press, 1974.

Tompkins, J. M. S., *The Popular Novel in England 1770–1800* (1932), London, Methuen, 1969.

Tracy, Ann B., *The Gothic Novel 1790–1830: Plot Summaries and Index to Motifs*, Lexington, University of Kentucky Press, 1981.

Twitchell, James B., 'Heathcliff as Vampire', *Southern Humanities Review* 11 (1977): 355–62.

Varma, Devendra P., *The Gothic Flame: Being a History of the Gothic Novel in England* (1957), New York, Russell & Russell, 1964.

Varnado, S. L., *Haunted Presence: The Numinous in Gothic Fiction*, Tuscaloosa and London, University of Alabama Press, 1987.

Veeder, William, 'Carmilla: The Arts of Repression', *Texas Studies in Literature and Language* 22 (1980): 197–223.

Watkins, Daniel P., 'Social Hierarchy in Matthew Lewis's *The Monk*', *Studies in the Novel* 18 (1986): 115–24.

Wiesenfarth, Joseph, *Gothic Manners and the Classic English Novel*, Madison and London, Uuniversity of Wisconsin Press, 1988.

Wilt, Judith, *Ghosts of the Gothic: Austen, Eliot and Lawrence*, Princeton, Princeton University Press, 1980.

——— , 'The Imperial Mouth: Imperialism, the Gothic and Science Fiction', *Journal of Poular Culture* 14 (1981): 618–28.

Wolf, Leonard, *The Annotated Dracula*, New York, Clarkson N. Potter, 1975.